CONCILIUM

concilium 1993/5

REINCARNATION OR RESURRECTION?

Edited by

Hermann Häring and
Johann-Baptist Metz

SCM Press · London
Orbis Books · Maryknoll

Published by SCM Press Ltd, 26–30 Tottenham Road, London N1
and by Orbis Books, Maryknoll, NY 10545

October 1993

ISBN: 0 334 03021 8 (UK)
ISBN: 0 88344 873 4 (USA)

Typeset at The Spartan Press Ltd, Lymington, Hants
Printed by Mackays of Chatham, Kent

Concilium Published February, April, June, August, October, December

Contents

Editorial

Reincarnation or Resurrection? A Discussion Reopened

Can we hope for more than just an earthly life? Must we fear many lives? Is there a spiritual element in us (whether we call it spirit, soul, Atman or Jiva) which survives our death, and time and again enters into the flesh of an earthly life? For centuries Christian theology has only thought about these questions in passing, if at all. Thinkers like Origen and Augustine still grappled with a cycle of life. Otherwise the early church tended to find this idea curious, since gradually Christian anthropology found another way forward for human beings. This way begins with a unique birth, leads through a *unique life* to an unrepeatable death and finally to an eternal life that leaves us entirely to God's will, which decides our future. Certainly, the models of Christian eschatology differed, and differ, in detail. For example, problems were caused by the time between individual death and the end of history, the possibility of a purgatory between heaven and hell, indeed the very possibility of a hell. But one thing was always clear for Christian theology: we have one life and it cannot be repeated. God lets us go our way once, and we have to make use of this opportunity. However, anyone who does forfeit his or her opportunity (as most do) can and should hope for God's grace.

Does this refute the notion of reincarnation? So far it has certainly not succeeded in doing so. Not only the adherents of Hindu religions and Buddhism, in other words around one billion people, accept it, but in a great many variations in African and Latin American religions so too do people who are deeply bound up with ancestors, nature, or both together. Nor should we forget the countless new syncretistic forms of religion which are gaining a new footing in industrialized countries. Mention should be made not only of theosophy and anthroposophy but also of systems which we usually describe as 'spiritism', 'occultism', 'new age' or 'esoteric spirituality'. Finally, it is worth reflecting that the notion of reincarnation is also fascinating Christians in Western countries in an unexpected way.

How are we to interpret this phenomenon? Is the Christianization of the idea of reincarnation necessary, or at least possible? Can the migration of the nucleus of an 'I' from one body to another even be proved empirically? In any attempt to answer this question we should allow ourselves to be guided by three starting points.

First, the discussion should be carried on in a spirit of dialogue. Dialogue does not exclude one's own decisive position. But it requires that we give the notion of reincarnation a religious status and recognize the possibility that it can help towards solving religious problems.

Secondly, instead of appealing in authoritarian fashion to our own tradition, we must enter into a substantive discussion, since an intensive critical discussion has not yet been carried on. The centuries-long absence of a problem could become a trap, as has been the case in countless other questions.

Thirdly, we must guard against objectifying ideas about reincarnation too hastily from the perspective of the onlooker and identifying them with banalities. Was I once a rat and will I become a pig? Of course these are realistic pictures, as Christians also have realistic pictures of heaven. But we also know their limitations. We can never catch the existential mood, the utopian force and the ethical bond in religious symbols through descriptions. That is true not only of the resurrection of the dead but also of reincarnation.

Anyone who accepts these starting points will soon become aware how tremendously complex the discussion is. No religious symbol speaks just through itself; it takes on its precise significance only in connection with other statements. That is true to an even greater degree of reincarnation. So the discussion has to be carried on at a great variety of levels. Here are some questions and experiences from which the notion of reincarnation draws its religious force.

We are moved by the question of the origin and future of human beings. Do we come from nothing and return to nothing? And is not the answer to this question connected with our notion of 'nothing', which can represent an endless cycle, show the limits of religious fulfilment or even comprise the negation of all being? One has only to compare the 'nothing' of the biblical idea of creation with Buddha's 'Nirvana'.

We are moved by injustice and evil in the world, the inequality between individuals and the impossibility of avoiding suffering and grief. Is there a reason for this which does not lie in God but in ourselves? Some articles will show how intensively the idea of reincarnation is bound up with the question of theodicy.

We are moved by the bond with our ancestors, with friends and loved ones beyond death. Can we count on their fellowship, hope for their protection, delight in their presence?

Then we know the notion of a way of purification on which we assimilate earlier action (whether guilty or not), all reference to the I (whether egotistical or not) and superficiality. Cannot a return into the wider context of the cosmos be a solution? This religious expectation forms the central and almost royal argument for reincarnation.

Finally there is the experience of opportunities wasted, of our own limits and the many possibilities which cannot be fulfilled in one life. Must it not be possible for a finite being to grow much more in his or her being than is possible in the few years of a life?

However, the last notion shows how different the status of the idea of reincarnation can be. What in India is experienced in great seriousness as a painful way, namely that cycle that never wants to end, appears in the West, with its delight in evolution, as a way to personal consummation. What in other cultures leads to great communication with the dead, in the West turns into an almost painful curiosity about one's own past. The status of reincarnation is in fact deeply interwoven with notions of human beings and their individuality, of matter and spirit, of a cyclical or extended understanding of the world-age. Finally, reincarnation is deeply immersed in a particular picture of the Absolute, which is silent or acts, grants or forgives, remains the unnameable or becomes the passionately loving God. What follows from this? The present issue can do no more than start a discussion. The notion of reincarnation is too woven into religious experience for us to be able to open it up rapidly. Perhaps only those who believe in it can understand it; perhaps it will become fruitful for Christians only in cultures which bear its stamp. There is also evidence of this in the present issue.

We begin the discussion with an alternative, the counter-image which in Christian tradition answers the questions we have raised. We found it in the message of resurrection, which stamps Christian belief from the start. Resurrection, too, gives an answer to the question of our future, the injustice and evil in the world, the sense of separation and grief. It too takes in the forgiveness of guilt and promises a bond with loved ones beyond their death. In resurrection we are guaranteed the reconciliation of humankind. Finally, resurrection reconciles us with our own limitations, because of which we do not deserve access to salvation.

But resurrection, too, escapes any objective description. Only those understand it who can give themselves over to death and have gone 'to the other side of the mountain'. As Pohier remarks, Christian faith does not offer any other answers, but puts the questions in another context. That is what this issue is ultimately about. In three passages in the *City of God* (in books X, XI and XII) Augustine went into the question more closely. However, he never reflects on the conception in itself but always on time: for him this is the decisive context which has also proved decisive in this issue. God's time is unique, filled, directed and finally completed time. The notion of endless becoming loses its religious force in this eschatological notion.

But can one not argue the other way round – so that the cycle of time extends the hope of resurrection so to speak to an endlessly last point in time? Certainly, there may and will be arguments about that, but at least that gives the discussion a central theme. For the analysis of time not only leads to an appropriate understanding of reincarnation but also accentuates the understanding of Christian resurrection. It shows that an anthropology beyond time and beyond history fails to do justice to the original impulse as much as does the idea of an eternal and immortal soul, at whose end time is as it were brought to a standstill. No, the resurrection of the dead actively puts an end to world time. Therefore resurrection acts as a provocation, not as the natural consequence of a religious concept. Christians too have to learn this again. At all events the cycle is broken. Whatever the past may have been, Augustine thinks, it is decisive for us 'that we should experience something new, something great and splendid, of a kind that we have not experienced before' (*City of God* XI, 5).

Hermann Häring
Johann Baptist Metz

I · Information on Ideas of Reincarnation

Reincarnation in Hinduism

Wendy Doniger

There are many different approaches to death and rebirth in the Hindu tradition, offering many different non-solutions to the insoluble problem, many different ways that the square peg of the fact of death cannot be fitted into the round hole of human rationality. These approaches are often aware of one another; they react against one another and incorporate one another, through the process of intertextuality. A survey of Hindu thinking about reincarnation can therefore offer us many new ways to think about our own ideas about death and, indeed, about our own deaths.

1. Death in the *Rig Veda*

The earliest extant Indian text, the *Rig Veda*, composed in North-West India around 1000 BCE, regards death as an inevitable part of chaos, something to be avoided as long as possible. The poet says, speaking of the Creator, 'His shadow is immortality – and death,'[1] and he prays, 'Deliver me from death, not from immortality.'[2] By 'immortality' the ancient sages meant not a literal eternity of life but rather a full life-span, reckoned as a hundred years. And when it comes to the inevitable end of that brief span, the *Rig Veda* offers varied but not necessarily contradictory images of a vague but pleasant afterlife, a rather muted version of life on earth.

One funeral hymn addresses the dead man:

> Go forth, go forth on those ancient paths on which our ancient fathers passed beyond . . . Unite with the fathers, with Yama [king of the dead], with the rewards of your sacrifices and good deeds, in the highest heaven. Leaving behind all imperfections, go back home again; merge with a glorious body.[3]

But, despite this 'glorious body' with which the dead person unites, another hymn expresses concern that the old body be preserved, and confidence that this will be so. The hymn begins by addressing the funeral fire, Agni:

> Do not burn him entirely, Agni, or engulf him in your flames. Do not consume his skin or his flesh. When you have cooked him perfectly, only then send him forth to the fathers.[4]

Not only is the fire not to destroy the body, but it is to preserve it. Speaking to the dead man, the hymn says:

> Whatever the black bird has pecked out of you, or the ant, the snake, or even a beast of prey, may Agni who eats all things make it whole . . .[5]

But it also speaks, again to the dead man, of the ultimate dispersal of the old body:

> May your eye go to the sun, your life's breath to the wind. Go to the sky or to earth, as is your nature; or go to the waters, if that is your fate. Take root in the plants with your limbs.[6]

Another hymn says to the dead man:

> Creep away to this broad, vast earth, the mother that is kind and gentle.

And to the earth:

> Open up, earth; do not crush him. Be easy for him to enter and to burrow in. Earth, wrap him up as a mother wraps a son in the edge of her skirt.[7]

Thus, even at this early stage, we have several rather different, but all relatively mild, views of the fate of the dead, views which seem to represent several degrees of rebirth. We might rank these options on a continuum from the most vivid to the least vivid: the dead man may somehow merge with a glorious body, presumably (but not necessarily) in heaven; his mortal body may be somehow purified and restored by the fire and united with his ancestors (again, presumably in heaven); the parts of his body may be dispersed to the elements of the cosmos; or he may return to the kindly womb of mother earth. Nowhere, however, is it explicitly said that he is to be reborn on earth in any form.

2. Redeath in the Brahmanas

In the texts that follow the *Rig Veda* and gloss it, the Brahmanas (c. 900 BC), death is far more explicitly feared, but also more explicitly transcended. 'Evil Death' is a cliché, an automatic equation throughout this corpus: death is evil, and the essence of evil is death. The fear of death, and the obsessive search for rituals that can overcome it, is the central concern of the Brahmanas.[8] At first it is said that only the gods can become immortal: 'The gods dispelled evil from them and are set free from death; though the sacrificer cannot obtain immortality, he attains the full measure of life.'[9] But when this text repeats almost the same sentiment, it suddenly adds that the sacrificer does in fact 'become immortal'.[10]

How does the sacrificer become literally immortal? One text of this genre includes, but also overcomes, what appears to be a circular logic of ritualism:

> When the Creator was creating living beings, evil Death overpowered him. He performed asceticism for a thousand years, striving to leave that evil behind him, and in the thousandth year he purified himself entirely; the evil that he washed clean in his body. But what man could obtain a life of a thousand years? The man who knows this truth can obtain a thousand years.[11]

This last phrase is a variant of the basic *Leitmotif* of the Brahmanas: 'Whoever knows this conquers death.'

Another Brahmana contains a very early foreshadowing of the doctrine of rebirth, though probably this is still rebirth in some extraterrestrial Vedic world, not yet the rebirth on earth that will be the innovation of the Upanishads:

> Death, the Ender, goes to the end of the life-span of mortals by means of day and night, so that they die. And if someone knows that Death, the Year, is the Ender, the Ender does not go to the end of his life-span by means of day and night before old age, and so he lives out a full life-span.
>
> The gods were afraid of this Ender, Death; they thought, 'Let him not go to the end of our life-spans by means of day and night.' They performed the sacrificial rituals and became immortal. Death said to the gods, 'All men will become immortal in precisely this way, and then what share will be mine?' They said, 'From now on, no one else will become immortal together with the body. But as soon as you have taken (the body as) your share, then, after separating from his body, he will become immortal – if he is someone who has achieved immortality

through knowledge or through action (*karma*).' And those who have this knowledge, or who do this ritual, they come to life again when they have died, and as soon as they come to life again they come to immortal life. But those who do not have this knowledge or who do not do this ritual, when they die they come to life again, but they become the food of this (Death) again and again.[12]

An expanded form of the usual final promise states, 'Whoever knows this conquers *recurring death* and attains a full life-span; this is freedom from death in the other world and life here.'[13] The phrase 'recurring death' or 'redeath' (*punar mrtyu*) is an essential key to our understanding of the Hindu attitude to reincarnation. To Western thinkers, reincarnation seems to pose a possible solution to the problem of death: if what you fear is the cessation of life (we will set aside for the moment considerations of heaven and hell), then the belief that you will, in fact, live again after you die may be of comfort: how nice to go around again and again, never to be blotted out altogether, to have more and more of life, different lives all the time. This being so, the fact that, as we shall see, a major school of Hindu (and Buddhist) philosophy strives *not* to be reborn, strives to attain freedom (*moksha*) from ever being born again, has struck many Western thinkers as a pessimistic or nihilistic attitude: such Hindus (the Western critic reasons) are throwing away not merely the present life but all those potential future lives as well, commiting a kind of multiple suicide.

But this line of reasoning entirely misses the point of the Hindu doctrine. What the authors of the Brahmanas feared was not life but death – more precisely, 'old age and death' (*jaramrtyu*). And what they feared most of all was what they called 'recurrent death'. This may have meant merely a series of ritual deaths within a natural life-span[14] or what T. S. Eliot had in mind when he said, 'We die to each other each day'. But it may have foreshadowed an actual series of rebirth and redeaths. As the text cited above states, 'When they die they come to life again, but they become the food of this (Death) again and again.' And if it is a terrible thing to grow old and die, once and for all, how much more terrible to do it over and over again?

3. Rebirth in the Upanishads

The Brahmanas' fear of death, single or repeated, led to an entirely different approach to death in the texts that follow, and gloss, the Brahmanas: the Upanishads, composed from about 700 BCE. Like the

Brahmanas, the Upanishads speak of redeath (*punarmyrtyu*) long before they begin speaking of rebirth (*punarjanma*). The Buddha, preaching at roughly the same time, taught that misery (*duhkha*) is not so much suffering as the inevitable loss of happiness, a chaos from which *nirvana* (the Buddhist equivalent of *moksha*) offered the solution. This recurrent loss of happiness is the problem faced by the Upanishads, the problem of redeath. The Upanishads reverse the Rig Vedic equation of death with chaos, life with order, and state, instead, that life (sex, birth, what Kazantzakis's Zorba called 'the whole disaster') is chaos, a dream, or rather a nightmare, while death (or final release from life, *moksha*) is order, a dreamless sleep. From the very start, the idea that transmigration occurred was immediately followed by two other ideas: that it was possible for some people to get free of it, and that it was desirable for some people to get free of it.

Though, as we have seen, there are tantalizing precursors of a doctrine of rebirth in the Brahmanas and even in the *Rig Veda*, the first explicit discussion of the doctrine of rebirth in Indian literature occurs in the Upanishads. A king asks a young man named Gautama (no relation to the Buddha) if he knows the answer to the following questions:

> 'Do you know where created beings go from here?' 'No, sir.' 'Do you know how they come back again?' 'No, sir.' 'Do you know about the separation between the two paths, the path of the gods and the path of the fathers?' 'No, sir.' 'Do you know how the world (of heaven) over there does not get filled up?' 'No, sir.' 'Do you know how, in the fifth oblation, water comes to have a human voice?' 'No, sir.'

And eventually the king tells the boy the answers:

> When the embryo has lain inside the womb for ten months or nine months, or however long, covered with the membrane, then he is born. When he is born, he lives as long as his allotted life-span. When he has died, they carry him to the appointed place and put him in the fire, for that is where he came from, what he was born from.
>
> Those who know this, and those who worship in the forest, concentrating on faith and asceticism, they are born into the flame, and from the flame into the day, and from the day into the fortnight of the waxing moon, and from the fortnight of the waxing moon into the six months during which the sun moves north; from these months, into the year; from the year into the sun; from the sun into the moon, from the moon into lightning. There a Person who is not human leads them to the ultimate reality. This is the path that the gods go on.

But those who worship in the village, concentrating on sacrifices and good works and charity, they are born into the smoke, and from the smoke into the night, and from the night into the other fortnight, and from the other fortnight into the six months when the sun moves south. They do not reach the year. From these months they go to the world of the fathers, and from the world of the fathers to space, and from space to the moon. That is king Soma. That is the food of the gods. The gods eat that.

When they have dwelt there for as long as there is a remnant (of their merit), then they return along that very same road that they came along, back into space; but from space they go to wind, and when one has become wind he becomes smoke, and when he has become smoke he becomes mist; when he has become mist, he becomes a cloud, and when he has become a cloud, he rains. These are then born here as rice, barley, plants, trees, sesame plants, and beans. It is difficult to move forth out of this condition; for whoever eats him as food and then emits him as semen, he becomes that creature's semen and is born.

And so those who behave nicely here will, in general, find a nice womb, the womb of a Brahmin or the womb of a Kshatriya or the womb of a Vaishya. But those whose behaviour here is stinking will, in general, find a stinking womb, the womb of a dog or the womb of a pig or the womb of an Untouchable. Then they become those tiny creatures who go by neither one of these two paths but are constantly returning. 'Be born and die'–that is the third condition. And because of that, the world (of heaven) over there is not filled up. And one should try to protect oneself from that . . . Whoever knows this becomes pure, purified, and wins a world of merit, if he really knows this.[15]

It would seem from this famous text that one would want to 'know this' and to 'protect oneself from that'. But in fact, a less well known early Upanishad also clearly envisions the possibility that some people will *not* want to get out: when the soul of the dead man reaches the moon, he may be given a choice of continuing with the process of rebirth or getting out altogether (*moksha*), and the text states that some people will choose to be reborn.[16] These two tracks – one for people who *want* to get off the wheel, and one for those who don't – continue to this day as options for South Asians, who all assume that we are all on the wheel of redeath, transmigration (*samsara*), but who do not at all agree whether it is good or bad to be on the wheel, or how best to go about getting off it if one does want to get off.[17]

4. Reincarnation in the Puranas

In the mediaeval period, c. 500–1,000 CE, the philosophical concept of reincarnation developed in the Upanishads were fleshed out, as it were, in narratives about reincarnation. One set of myths pits death against withdrawal from life altogether, focusing upon the great god of ascetics, yogis, and renouncers: Siva. All of the variants of this particular network of myths begin with the same premise: the Creator asks Siva to create living creatures. In the first set of stories, so great is Siva's pity for creatures who would utimately be subject to redeath that he refuses to create any creatures at all, engaging in a kind of prophylactic euthanasia, and the Creator gets another god to make the flawed creatures who are our ancestors. In a second set of variations, Siva engages in yoga in order to create immortals,[18] but either (subvariant a) he takes too long, and the Creator in his impatience creates us; or (subvariant b), when Siva produces a kind of trial run of twelve immortals identical with himself, they prove to be so arrogant and destructive that the Creator refuses to let Siva continue the line, and has someone else create us.[19]

Other texts from this period enact the implications of the theory of *karma* (action), the theory that the actions that a person commits in life, for better or worse, leave traces on the soul, and the nature of these traces will determine the nature of that person's rebirth. Some of these texts emphasize the moral self-loathing of the reincarnating soul:

> In the womb, the embryo begins to remember its many previous existences in the wheel of rebirth, and that depresses it, and it tosses from side to side, thinking, 'I won't ever do *that* again, as soon as I get out of this womb. I will do everything I can, so that I won't become an embryo again.' It thinks in this way as it remembers the hundreds of miseries of birth that it experienced before, in the power of fate.
>
> Then, as time goes by, the embryo turns around, head down, and in the ninth or tenth month it is born. As it comes out, it is hurt by the wind of procreation; it comes out crying, because it is pained by the misery in its heart. When it has come out of the womb, it falls into an unbearable swoon, but it regains consciousness when it is touched by the air. Then Vishnu's deluding power of illusion assails him, and when his soul has been deluded by it, he loses his knowledge. As soon as the living creature has lost his knowledge, he becomes a baby.
>
> After that he becomes a young boy, then an adolescent, and then an old man. And then he dies and then he is born again as a human. Thus he wanders on the wheel of rebirth like the bucket on the wheel of a well.[20]

As if this were not bad enough, there is also the matter of hell. As we have seen, the *Rig Veda* already has a vague idea of heaven; it also has a rather vague idea of hell. Later Hindu mythology, with its inevitable tendency to the rococo, elaborated upon these relatively simple cosmologies and posited many heavens and many hells, a *mandala* of retribution that makes Dante's world look like child's play. A Western reader might think that the cyclic concept of reincarnation would obviate any need, or indeed any use, for a heaven or hell in which one would be rewarded or punished for all eternity, but this is not the case. The older Vedic idea of heaven and hell was simply folded into the newer Upanishadic idea of rebirth, much as the older, Indo-European idea of linear time (the four Ages of steadily declining virtue) was folded into the later Hindu idea of cyclical time (creation followed by doomsday followed by creation . . .): it was simply said that after the fourth Age came doomsday, then creation, then the first Age, then the fourth Age . . .

This was how the combination worked: we have already seen, in the Upanishads, a bifurcation or dichotomy in the cycle of reincarnation: reincarnating souls go either to the flame, the sun, and finally to freedom or ultimate reality; or to the smoke, the moon, and the cycle of rebirth. In the case of heaven/hell and rebirth, it was simply said that after death, the reincarnating soul takes one of two paths: if good *karma* predominates over bad *karma*, the soul goes first to hell for a relatively brief period, where it works out or consumes its bad *karma* by being tormented, and then to heaven for a long period, where it enjoys the fruits of its good *karma*. If bad *karma* predominates, the soul goes first briefly to heaven and then for a longer sojourn in hell. In either case, after the two sorts of *karma* are consumed, the soul is reborn in a station in life determined by the original balance of good and evil *karma*.

5. Reincarnation in later Hindu mythology and philosophy

Hindus continued to tell stories and to develop theories about reincarnation, many of them expressed in a kind of mixed genre of philosophical narrative whose masterpiece is the *Yogavasistha*, a text composed in Sanskrit in Kashmir in the tenth century of the Common Era.[21] There are many stories about reincarnation in this text, and one of the best (a very long text of which I can only sketch the outlines here) includes many detailed suggestions about the mechanisms that might determine the precise ways in which we are reborn:

Once upon a time there was a monk who was inclined to imagine things rather a lot. One day, he happened to imagine a man named Jivata, who drank too much and fell into a heavy sleep. As Jivata dreamt, he saw a Brahmin who read all day long. One day, that Brahmin fell asleep, and as his daily activities were still alive within him, like a tree inside a seed, he dreamt that he was a prince. One day that prince fell asleep after a heavy meal, and dreamt that he was a great king. One day that king fell asleep, having gorged himself on his every desire, and in his dream he saw himself as a celestial woman. The woman fell into a deep sleep in the languor that followed making love, and she saw herself as a doe with darting eyes. That doe one day fell asleep and dreamed that she was a clinging vine, because she had been accustomed to eating vines; for animals dream, too, and they always remember what they have seen and heard.

The vine saw herself as a bee that used to buzz among the vines; the bee fell in love with a lotus and was so intoxicated by the lotus sap he drank that his wits became numb; just then an elephant came to that pond and trampled the lotus, and the bee, still attached to the lotus, was crushed with it on the elephant's tusk. As the bee looked at the elephant, he saw himself as an elephant in rut. That elephant in rut fell into a deep pit and became the favorite elephant of a king. One day the elephant was cut to pieces by a sword in battle, and as he went to his final resting place he saw a swarm of bees hovering over the sweet ichor that oozed from his temples, and so the elephant became a bee again. The bee returned to the lotus pond and was trampled under the feet of another elephant, and just then he noticed a goose beside him in the pond, and so he became a goose. That goose moved through other births, other wombs, for a long time, until one day, when he was a goose in a flock of other geese, he realized that, being a goose, he was the same as the swan of the Creator. Just as he had this thought, he was shot by a hunter and he died, and then he was born as the swan of the Creator.

One day the swan saw God, and I thought, with sudden certainty, 'I am God.' Immediately that idea was reflected like an image in a mirror, and he took on the form of God. Then he could see all of his former experiences, and he understood them: 'Because Jivata admired Brahmins, he saw himself as a Brahmin; and since the Brahmin had thought about princes all the time, he became a prince. And that fickle woman was so jealous of the beautiful eyes of a doe that she became a doe . . . These creatures are my own rebirths.' And, after a while, the monk and Jivata and all the others will wear out their bodies and will unite in the world of God.[22]

The story goes on to raise other metaphysical issues, but for our purposes several important points are made here. The transition to a new life can take place either by thinking of something or by suffering a violent death, for dreaming and dying are conflated. Both dreaming and dying are brought on by over-indulgence in the pleasures of the senses, and those same pleasures of the senses determine the content of the dream or the new life. Indeed, sensual appeal is what attracts the soul to the next life: love, admiration (even, sometimes, in its negative aspect of jealousy), obsession, fascination. God himself (the supreme deity, who is regarded here, as often in Hindu mythology, as existing on a level that encompasses the tasks and powers of the Creator) is caught up in this round of attraction, but he is also the source of our own attractions, the source to which we return when the cycle has played itself out.

6. Reincarnation for non-Hindus

Although ideas about reincarnation have occurred in many cultures, South Asian civilization is usually regarded as the fountainhead of this belief. Thus, for example, to this day, South Asian evidence predominates in Ian Stevenson's multi-volume, cross-cultural, scientific investigations of reincarnation.[23] How are we in the West to come to terms with this belief? Is it for them? Is it for us?

I myself gradually came first to think with and then to feel with the *karma* theory. The *karma* theory *tells* us that we have lived other lives, that our souls have had other bodies. But how can we *feel*, as well as accept intellectually, the reality of those other lives if we cannot remember them? For us who are not Hindus, the previous incarnation unrecalled has no existence. For some things in life can be remembered in one's soul, but other things can only be remembered with one's body.

The body remembers some things, and the mind remembers others. But memory is not all there is; there is also a reality of unrecalled experience that gives a kind of validity to our connection with lives that we do not recall. The *karma* theory recognizes the parallelism between events forgotten within a single life – the events of early childhood, or the things that we repress or that (in Indian mythology) we forget as the result of a curse[24] – and the events forgotten from a previous life. It also recognizes a similarity in the ways in which we sometimes half-recall these various sorts of events, often with a sense of *déjà vu*. We remember something that we cannot remember, from a lost past, through the power of the invisible tracks or traces left behind on our souls by those events; these traces the Hindus call perfumes (*vasanas*).[25]

The *karma* theory tells us that we have lived lives that we cannot remember and hence cannot feel. But for those of us who lack the imagination to perceive the infinity of our lives in time, it might be possible to perceive the infinity of our lives in human space. Again, the Indian texts tell us that we are karmically linked to all the other people in the world; they *are us*. I have known and respected this theory for a long time, though I have not always believed it.[26] But for one important moment, I did believe it. It was at a time when I was feeling rather sorry for myself for having only one child; I wished that I had had lots of children, and now it was too late. I felt that having six children would have meant having an entirely different life, not merely six times the life of a woman with one child, and I wanted that life as well as the life that I had. This thought was in my mind as I wandered on a beach in Ireland, and saw a woman with lots and lots of children, very nice children, too, and at their best, as young children often are on a beach. Normally, I would have envied her; but this time, I enjoyed her children. I was happy to watch them. And suddenly I felt that they were mine, that the woman on the beach had had them for me, so that they would be there for me to watch them as they played in the water. Her life was my life too; I felt it then, and I remember it now. What had been an idea to me until then, the idea of my karmic identity with other people, became an experience. I was able to live her life in my imagination.

One way of interpreting my epiphany of the woman on the beach was this realization that my connection to her – and, through her, to every other woman who had ever had or ever would have children – meant that my brief life-span was expanded into the life-spans of all the other people in the world. This is a very Hindu way of looking at one's relationship with all other people. Woven through the series of individual lives, each consisting of a cluster of experiences, was the thread of the experience itself – in this case, motherhood. That experience would survive when her children and mine were long dead.

I felt then that all the things that one wanted to do and to be existed in eternity; they stood there for ever, as long as there was human life on the planet Earth. They were like beautiful rooms that anyone could walk into; and when I could no longer walk into them, they would still be there. They were part of time, and though they could not go on being part of me for much longer, part of me would always be there in them. Something of me would still linger in those things that I had loved, like the perfume or pipe smoke that tells you that someone else has been in a room before you. This is the same 'perfume', the same karmic trace of memory, that adheres to the transmigrating soul. And through my connection with the woman on the beach, I would be the people in the future who sensed in that room the perfume that I had left behind, though (unless I was a gifted sage) I would not recognize it as my perfume. Perhaps, since I am not a Hindu, that is as close as I can come to believing that I can remember my other lives: remembering other peoples' lives as my life. And perhaps it is close enough.[27]

Notes

1. *Rig Veda*, 10.121.2; translation by Wendy Doniger O'Flaherty, *The Rig Veda: An Anthology*, Harmondsworth 1981, 27.

2. *Rig Veda*, 7.59.12.

3. *Rig Veda*, 10.14.7–8; O'Flaherty, *The Rig Veda*, 44.

4. *Rig Veda*, 10.16.1; O'Flaherty, *The Rig Veda*, 49.

5. *Rig Veda*, 10.16.6; O'Flaherty, *The Rig Veda*, 50.

6. *Rig Veda*, 10.16.3; O'Flaherty, *The Rig Veda*, 49.

7. *Rig Veda*, 10.18.10–11; O'Flaherty, *The Rig Veda*, 53.

8. See Wendy Doniger O'Flaherty, *Tales of Sex and Violence: Folklore, Sacrifice, and Danger in the Jaiminiya Brahmana*, Chicago 1985.

9. *Satapatha Brahmana*, Benares 1964, 2.1.3.4.

10. *Satapatha Brahmana*, 2.2.2.14. See Wendy Doniger O'Flaherty, *The Origins of Evil in Hindu Mythology*, Berkeley 1976, 215.

11. *Shatapatha Brahmana*, 10.4.4.1–3. Cited by O'Flaherty, *The Origins of Evil* (n.10), 217.

12. *Satapatha Brahmana*, 10.4.3.1–10, condensed.

13. *Satapatha Brahmana*, 10.2.6.19.

14. See Herman Tull, *The Vedic Origins of Karma*, Albany, New York 1989.

15. *Chandogya Upanishad*, 5.3.1–10. See Wendy Doniger O'Flaherty, *Textual Sources for the Study of Hinduism*, Chicago 1990, 35–7. See also *Brihadaranyaka Upanishad*, 4.4.

16. *Kaushitaki Upanishad*, 1.1–7.

17. This is not the time or place to discuss the problems in the *karma* solution to the problem of death, problems that I have raised elsewhere. See Wendy Doniger O'Flaherty, *Karma and Rebirth in Classical Indian Traditions*, Berkeley 1980.

18. For a discussion of yoga as a means of overcoming death, see Mircea Eliade, *Yoga: Immortality and Freedom*, New York 1958.

19. See Wendy Doniger O'Flaherty, *Siva: The Erotic Ascetic*, London 1973 and New York 1986, 130–8.

20. *Markandeya Purana*, Bombay 1890, 10.1–7; 11.1–21; O'Flaherty, *Textual Sources* (n.15), 98.

21. See Wendy Doniger O'Flaherty, *Dreams, Illusion, and Other Realities*, Chicago 1984.

22. *Yogavasistha-Maha-Ramayana*, ed. W. L. S. Pansikar (2 vols.), Bombay 1918, 6.1.62–69; O'Flaherty, *Dreams* (n.21), 207–8, and 'The Dream Narrative and the Indian Doctrine of Illusion', *Daedalus*, Summer 1982, 93–113.

23. Ian Stevenson, *Twenty Cases Suggestive of Reincarnation*, Charlottesville, Va. 1966; *Cases of the Reincarnation Type* (4 vols.), Charlottesville, Va. 1975–1983; *Children Who Remember Previous Lives*, Charlottesville, Va. 1987.

24. Robert P. Goldman, 'Karma, Guilt, and Buried Memories: Public Fantasy and Private Reality in Traditional India', *Journal of the American Oriental Society* 105, 3, 1985, 413–25.

25. A similar concept of physical traces on the transmigrating soul may be seen in Plato's *Gorgias* 524, in which a man who has been whipped bears the marks of the whip upon him when he is judged after his death.

26. My belief in the *karma* theory was, wrongly, challenged by Goldman in 'Karma, Guilt, and Buried Memories'.

27. This passage is condensed from Wendy Doniger O'Flaherty, *Other Peoples' Myths: The Cave of Echoes*, New York 1988, 14–15.

Reincarnation in Buddhism: A Christian Appraisal

Aloysius Pieris

1. The specificity of the Buddhist theory

Buddhism does not admit a soul that transmigrates from body to body. What links two lives is *viññāna* or consciousness, a mental process. Not being an immortal soul, it is *continuous but not absolutely identical* with what existed in the previous life, so that reincarnation really means 're-becoming' (*punabbhava*). Hence, what is reborn is neither the same nor another (*na ca so na ca añño*).

If Hellenism is what makes our theology require an immortal soul to account for an individual's postmortem survival, it would be illuminating to compare the way St Paul explains 'resurrection' to his Greek congregation in Corinth[1] with the way the Buddhist apologete Nagasena explains the notion of re-becoming to his Greek interlocutor Milinda (Menander) about a century or more earlier.[2]

They both resort to the simile of the seed which dies and the tree which grows out of it. The one is, in some way, continuous with the other, and yet they are not the same. Neither Paul nor Nagasena speaks of some permanent non-physical entity which continues as the guarantor of personal identity and another physical element that joins it in the coming life. Their respective anthropologies did not include that hypothesis.

Obviously, 'resurrection from the dead' and reincarnation are not of the same soteriological order. The resurrection is the final and total liberation, the ultimate realization of God's Reign; re-becoming, on the other hand, points to the very absence of 'final release'. For, Nirvana is the cessation of both death and rebirth; it is freedom from re-becoming.

Furthermore, in rebirth, the body perishes while consciousness continues as a series of psychic moments in another perishable body. But resurrection for Paul is the death of *sarx*, the perishable body (i.e., the perishable *person*), and the rise of *soma pneumatikon*, a spiritually transformed body (i.e., an imperishable *person*).

2. Rebirth and the intermediary existence

Roman Catholic theology appeals to scriptures (Luke 23.43; Rev. 6.9; 20.4), even to Paul (Phil. 1.21 and II Cor. 5.6–8) in support of an intermediary existence between one's death and one's resurrection – a stage in which the immortal soul lives in an ethos of being 'at home' with Christ.[3] This takes us to the doctrine of purgatory.

Some Catholic and non-Catholic Christians who are in dialogue with Buddhists have tried to reinterpret this doctrine of purgatory in terms of the Buddhist theory of re-becoming.[4] For the Buddhist, rebirth implies many a dip into the ocean of cosmic experience before reaching the meta-cosmic state of nirvana. Hence the question to the Christian: what if one needs more lives than one to grow into the full stature of Christian maturity which would climax in the resurrection? Could the cleansing effect of purgatory be seen more as the pain of spiritual growth than as mere punishment?

In most Asian seminaries we were taught that reincarnation was condemned by the *magisterium*. But the documents cited merely teach that eternal reward and eternal punishment follow immediately after death, except for souls that need further purgation.[5] The manner of purgation, however, is left unexplained. Reincarnation may not be the question directly addressed in such magisterial pronouncements.

In the anathemas against Origen – there is now a doubt about their authoritative nature[6] – what is directly attacked is the belief in the pre-existence of human souls[7] and not the theory of reincarnation *per se*. The Buddhists will whole-heartedly agree with that anathema!

3. A theological appropriation of the theory of rebirth?

Among the theological objections raised against the theory of reincarnation, only one merits an answer from a Buddhist point of view: how could I, or why should I, suffer the consequences of past actions of which I am not conscious now?

Beneath this objection lies the minimalist theory of imputability derived from the Roman jurisprudential theology of guilt and justification: that only an *actus humanus* (an action performed with full knowledge and consent) can be sinful. Such minimalism does not explain the whole mystery of sin, especially the burdens we humans carry as consequences of what we have allowed to happen in the deepest zones of our unconsciousness.

In Buddhism, ignorance (*avidya*) is the matrix of our sinful behaviour. The reality of sin goes deep into the realm of the subconscious where our real self is enslaved by it. Ignorance, far from exculpating a person, clamours for liberation through authentic knowledge which Buddhist spirituality offers to its practitioners. The Bible, too, mentions unconscious sins as needing forgiveness.[8] What about the 'serpent dimension' of sin which lurks in the depths of one's being before the actual fall (Gen. 3.1ff.)?

In an Asian theology, therefore, rebirth is bound to be taken seriously, if no dogma appears to be compromised thereby. Then our doctrine of purgatory would point to an intermediary stage of purificatory maturation mediated by many lives. Teilhard de Chardin's incorporation of the hypothesis of cosmic evolution into the theology of creation and redemption within the framework of Christogenesis seems to serve as a helpful precedent. If the cosmos is the evolving body of Christ, does the transformation of this perishable body into the glorious one require a full human participation in experiencing the length, the breadth, the height and the depth of this evolving [cosmic body of] Christ?

But how fruitful is this speculation if the scientific basis and rational consistency of the rebirth theory is weak?

The late Rev. Lynn A. de Silva – a Methodist theologian and a pioneer in Buddhist-Christian dialogue, who tried to bridge the theological distance between the doctrines of purgatory and rebirth – looked carefully into the cases of reincarnation so far adduced by Hindus and Buddhists and came to the conclusion that most of these case-studies fail the test of rigorous scientific analysis either because of inadequacies in the investigatory methods or the inability to exclude other possible explanations of the same phenomena, and, most of all, because of the unrepeatability of such investigations.[9]

With de Silva, I conclude tentatively that reincarnation is as much an object of faith for Buddhists as purgatory is for Catholics.

But there is an empirically verifiable facet of reincarnation which has not yet received proper theological attention, namely, the context that gave rise to the Buddhist idea of rebirth. Here our reflection could be more fruitful and less speculative.

4. The context: the search for immortality

Buddhism arose in the mid-country (modern Bihar) in the mid-sixth century BCE, when the old order was being challenged by a new one.[10] The old order was created by the Aryan immigrants who moved down the Indo-Gangetic plains since the second millennium BCE. By mid-sixth century, these cattle-breeding nomadic tribes had gradually settled down in villages they themselves had created. Theirs was a rural and tribal world-view which fostered a *cosmic* religiosity. By this I mean that their spiritual experience was characterized by a sacred this-worldliness.

The first part of the Hindu Scriptures – the *Veda* and the corresponding *Brahmana* literature – reflects this cosmic religiosity. Its outstanding characteristic was the centrality of the household – the sacred space in which marriage and sacrifice became the cultic focus of socio-cultural and politico-economic organization. The whole creation issued from Prajapati's primordial sacrifice; marriage thus became the supreme sacrificial ritual which perpetuates creation through procreation. In that world–view, therefore, *immortality is the physical continuation of the father in his own offspring*: 'In your offspring you are born again; that, O mortal, is your immortality',[11] as the Brahmana texts repeatedly say.[12]

Many are the implications of this world-view. The first is that immortality is *cosmic*, because it amounts to one's postmortem continuity here on earth through one's own offspring. Immortality, in other words, is one's repeated *rebirth* in this world, and in one's own progeny. The procreative act is the sacrificial rite (*karma*) which brings about this cosmic immortality. What dies is the individual, so to say, but what is reborn perpetuates the house-hold, the family, the society. These constitute a well-knit social fabric maintained through a code of caste-obligations. The individual fades away into the group's collectivity.

The *Upanisads* – the latter part of the Hindu Scriptures – reveal the new paradigm that gradually emerged as a challenge to this Vedic world-view, presumably, under the influence of an urban elite, around the sixth century BCE. The extremely fertile mid-country (modern Bihar) where Buddhism arose almost during the same period was reaping the first fruits of an agricultural surplus, increased population, growth of trade, rise of rival kingdoms leading to warfare and violence, and above all the spread of cities with unforeseen problems such as epidemics.

These changes brought with them a massive spiritual unrest, calling for – and eventually generating – a 'paradigm-shift' of a drastic kind.

Numerous new religious currents were whirling in the cities; but the source of these new movements among the urban elite was the forest (*aranya*), the antipole of the village (*grama*) where the old Vedic order still prevailed. The forest was where many city people went in search of *liberation from the world*, the very world wherein the village culture acquired immortality. But immortality sought and found in the forest was *metacosmic*, i.e., beyond this world. This meant that all cosmic powers (gods) were demoted. The metacosmic is also metatheistic.

Secondly, the new quest guaranteed one's *individuality* as against the collectivity of the group. By renouncing the caste-bound social system and moving to the forest, not only men but women, too, could become free individuals. Even rebirth was an individual's roaming in the world, rather than a male's biological continuity in his offspring. Paradoxically, however, the Ground of Immortality was conceived as the One Absolute and Real Self, into which the individual self seemed to fade out of its illusory existence.

Thirdly, those entering that state of immortality would not be reborn here! For this created universe – wherein one's *rebirth* used to be a desired fruit of the Vedic *karma* (marital act) – is now dreaded as *samsara*, the evil round of birth, death and rebirth.

This involves the fourth major departure from the old system: marriage which was believed to generate immortality [of lineage] now gives way to celibacy as the guarantee of the deathless state. Put facetiously, 'below the navel immortality' yields to 'above the navel immortality'! Thus was sown the seed of Asian monasticism in a soil that has never lost its fertility since then.

Note, finally, the shift of meaning in the notion of *karma*, the ritual action which pervaded the cosmic spirituality of the Vedic village. Continuity in this world – cosmic immortality, so to say – depended on that ritual performance. Now *karma* becomes the moral (rather than the ritual) action which determines whether one is reborn or not. Even moral action, however, needs to be transcended. What ultimately guarantees liberation is the salvific knowledge of the liberating Truth. The path of gnosis (*jñāna-mārga*) leads to immortality, not the path of ritualism (*karma-mārga*).

5. Rebirth as a cosmic experience with a metacosmic horizon

The Vedic and Brahmanic literature with its predominantly cosmic religiosity as well as the Aranyaka and Upanisadic writings which stir a gnostic quest for a metacosmic immortality have both been deftly brought together to form one single corpus of Sacred Scriptures. Hinduism in its many and varied forms has continued to maintain this equilibrium between the cosmic and the metacosmic poles of Asian religiosity.

Buddhism, too, developed its own symbiosis of the two propensities, both in its Scriptures and in its popular traditions in all parts of Asia.[13] The Buddhist doctrine of rebirth, too, makes sense if we perceive the cosmic and the metacosmic orders, each according to its own sense or level of meaning.

In the absolute sense (*paramatthato*), there is no individual soul in the human person, nor is there an Absolute Soul constituting the ultimate reality. In the absolute sense, Nirvana is liberation itself. 'Liberator' (implying an Absolute Soul) or 'state of liberation' (implying a liberated soul) is not predicated of Nirvana. The Psalms of the Mystics reveal only the *fruit* of liberation.[14]

But in the conventional (*vyavahārika*) sense, one speaks of the empirical person with an empirical ego legitimately seeking greater freedom in the cosmic order of birth, death and rebirth. The climax of a being's cosmic evolution through many lives is the human state which alone can attain the metacosmic. Even gods (cosmic powers) have to be reborn as humans to reach Nirvana. In short, the human person is defined as a cosmic being capable of a metacosmic (*lokottara*) pursuit. Rebirth, therefore, constitutes the personal and cosmic struggle for total liberation.

The Buddhist masses are saturated with this soteriology thanks to the popular media that re-enact and depict the 'five hundred and fifty reincarnations' which prepared the future Buddha for his final release. In South East Asia, an 'ascending Buddhology' which emphasizes the human origin of the Buddha constitutes the framework of a folk catechesis wherein rebirth is presented as an opportunity for spiritual progress through personal effort. The rebirth stories inculcate in the popular mind not only a personal devotion to the Buddha, but also the belief that all cosmic beings are orientated on a metacosmic horizon.

Teilhard de Chardin, who was notoriously impervious to Asian religiosity, caught the essence of this popular Buddhist vision when, according to his own admission, his veil of ignorance and prejudice was removed by an experienced missionary. Appreciating 'the old Buddhist preoccupation to sound the rhythm of the world, to establish a perspective of its countless evolutions, to await the supreme Buddha who is to redeem all things', he declared enthusiastically that we Christians should be 'more Buddhist' by discovering Christ as a 'Super-human Being' formed 'in the heart of the world'.[15]

Notes

1. I Cor 15. 35–37.
2. *Milinda's Questions* (translated by I. B. Horner), Vol. I, London 1990, 64, 98, 106.
3. See Joseph Schmid, 'Resurrection of the Body', *Sacramentum Mundi*, 1970, Vol.3, 340.
4. See Lynn A. de Silva, *Reincarnation in Buddhist and Christian Thought*, Colombo 1968, 161–3.
5. E.g. Denzinger 854, 1000 etc.; for Vatican II, see *Lumen Gentium* 49 and 51.
6. Norman Tanner, SJ, *Decrees of Ecumenical Councils*, London and Washington, DC 1990, Vol. I, 105–6.
7. I.e., *pro-huparchein tas ton anthropon psychas* (Denzinger 403).
8. E.g., Pss. 51.4–5; 19.12; Luke 23.34; I Tim. 1.13; etc.
9. De Silva. *Reincarnation* (n.4), 7–58.
10. In this section, I have summed up – with some additions and comments – the concise presentation given in Patrick Olivelle, *Sanyasa Upanisads. Hindu Scriptures on Asceticism and Renunciation*, New York 1992, 3–100.
11. Taittiriya Brahmana, 1.5.5.6, quoted in Olivelle, *Sanyusa Upanisads* (n.10), 27.
12. In that patriarchal set-up, the woman, as such, was not a ritual person; only the husband was, though not without his wife, who was merely the instrument in the ritual act of marriage by which immortality was sought through the progeny.
13. I have demonstrated this in *An Asian Theology of Liberation*, New York 1993, 71–4.
14. *Theragatha* and *Therigatha*, two canonical books of the Buddhist Scriptures.
15. *Letters to Leontine Zanta*, London 1969, 57–8.

Resurrection in the Intertestamental Literature and Rabbinic Theology

Hermann Lichtenberger

I. The Old Testament presuppositions

The presuppositions for the hope of resurrection in post-biblical Judaism lie in the Old Testament itself. Here we should think, in the wider sense, of the statements which speak of the God of Israel as the Lord over life and death, who is with his own even in death. That God's faithfulness lasts even beyond death is the certainty which gives hope of resurrection to those who are killed for the sake of this loyalty.

Before individual resurrection (see below, Dan.12) there are metaphorical statements about the resurrection of the shattered people which in Hos.6.1–4 are expressed in notions related to vegetation (cf. Isa.26.19–20, see below) and in Ezek.37.1–14 in imagery which presupposes ideas of overcoming the grave. As in ancient Greek notions, the dead continue to live a shadowy existence in the underworld (Hades, Sheol),[1] which consists in remoteness from God (Isa.38.11), the diminution of existence (Isa.14.10), indeed loss of consciousness (Eccles.9.5–6,10); the notion of sleep is also used (Job 3.13–18; 14.12). Where the boundary of death is reached in mortal sickness and the danger of death, rescue is experienced as rescue from death (C.Barth). The testimony to resurrection in Dan.12.1–3 can be defined with relative certainty both chronologically and in terms of content. The book of Daniel (which was composed shortly before 164) proclaims a transportation to the heavenly world after death for the martyrs killed in the Hellenistic religious persecution (12.3), and for the rest of Israel an 'awakening' to eternal life or disaster (12.2).

'And many of those who sleep in the dust
will awaken,
some to eternal life,
but the others to shame, to eternal disgrace.
But the teachers/wise will shine like
the stars in the firmament,
and those who have led many to righteousness
like the stars for ever and ever' (12.2–3).

There is certainly no thought in 12.2 of a general resurrection of all human beings, but of the resurrection of Israel to eternal life or to eternal disaster. It remains open in what way and at what place this will come about.

The transportation of the wise and the leaders of the faithful to the astral world has points of contact with Graeco-Hellenistic notions,[2] and continues to be influential (I Enoch 104.2); however, as Eccles.3.21 shows, it had already become a problem at an earlier stage.

Daniel 12.1–3 at the same time marks the transition to the literature of the post-biblical period, which at least in part is contemporaneous with some of the late writings.

II. Apocrypha and Pseudepigrapha of the Old Testament

This diverse literature speaks in a wide range of variations about resurrection and eternal life; it refers back to the biblical statements, but changes them under the influence of Hellenism.[3]

1. Ethiopian Enoch (I Enoch)

Closest chronologically to Daniel is Ethiopian Enoch (apart from the later Similitudes of chs.37–71), in which various expectations of what happens after death are juxtaposed.

First there is hope of resurrection for the righteous: 'The righteous will awaken from his sleep, and wisdom will raise herself up' (cf. 92.3–4; 23.13).

Secondly, chs.102–104 (cf. Wisdom 2–5) bewail the different fates of the souls of the righteous and the godless, although they suffer the same mortal fate:

'But you, souls of the righteous, fear not; and be hopeful, you souls that died in righteousness! Be not sad because your souls have gone down to Sheol in sorrow; or your flesh fared not well the earthly existence in accordance with your goodness' (102.4–5).

'The spirits of those who died in righteousness shall live and rejoice; their spirits shall not perish, nor their memorial from before the face of the Great One unto all the generations of the world' (103.4).

I Enoch develops the presuppositions for the different fates of the souls of the just and the godless in chs. 12–36, where in his journeys to heaven and the underworld Enoch is shown the abodes of the souls of the righteous and the places where the fallen angels and the souls of the godless are punished.

I Enoch 22.9–13 depicts three (or four) rooms: a room with a bright spring for the spirits of the just, two (or three) dark rooms for those of the sinners. One group of sinners will not be punished in the judgment, because they will not rise: the others, just and bad sinners, seem to be in an intermediate state until the judgment and the resurrection. 'In Dan. 12.2 and I Enoch 22 the resurrection is present in a double form, but it remains incomplete and does not apply to all the dead; I Enoch 27 removes the righteous and the damned to Jerusalem; the latter are punished in the valley of Hinnom in the presence of the righteous. Spiritualized and realistic conceptions stand side by side with relatively little connection.'[4]

In addition to the resurrection of the righteous and the godless there is the judgment (I Enoch 92–104), in which a decision will be made about their different fates. Here special significance is attached to heavenly books: they serve to list deeds (I Enoch 89.70, etc.) or as the book of life (Dan. 12.1).

2. II Maccabees

Whereas in Daniel and Ethiopian Enoch the form of the resurrection reality remains unclear, the martyr legends of II Maccabees expect a physical resurrection. While 6.26 shows merely the certainty of God's power in life and in death ('Whether I live or die I shall not escape the hands of the Almighty'), the martyrdom of the seven brothers in ch. 7 gives it concrete form. 'You accursed wretch, you dismiss us from this present life, but the King of the universe will raise us up to an everlasting renewal of life' (7.9; cf. 7.14). God will restore bread and life (7.23), indeed will materially restore limbs hacked off in torture (7.10). However, the wicked will experience no resurrection (7.14), but will be punished by God's judgment (7.36). Only Israel (all Israel?) will rise; the restitution of the multilated need not mean restoration of the same bodily nature. 12.43–45 shows that the resurrection hope was disputed and needed new arguments.

3. The Psalms of Solomon

Psalms of Solomon 3.12 speaks clearly of the resurrection of the righteous: 'Those who fear the Lord shall rise up to eternal life, and their life shall be in the Lord's light, and it shall never end'; evidently it is limited to the pious. The latter expectation is certainly to be understood in earthly terms, and possibly also the former.

4. The Testaments of the Twelve Patriarchs

The Testaments of the Twelve Patriarchs have the patriarchs talking both of their own future resurrection (TSim.6.7; TSeb.10.2) and of that of other fathers (TJud.25.1: Abraham, Isaac, Jacob; TBenj.10.6f.: Enoch, Noah, Shem, Abraham, Isaac and Jacob). The resurrection of the pious ('And those who died in sorrow shall be raised in joy; and those who died on account of the Lord shall be wakened to life', TJud.25.4) takes place in the time of salvation ('there shall no more be Beliar's spirit of error', TJud.25.3). With the resurrection of the forefathers and the twelve patriarchs the general resurrection of the dead takes place, 'some to glory and others to shame' (TBenj 10.8; cf. Dan.12.2). After the judgment on Israel and the Gentiles 'all Israel will be gathered to the Lord' (TBenj 10.11).

In the texts treated so far there are on the one hand disparate notions about existence after death and on the other hand often unclear, fluctuating statements about the resurrection of the dead.

The following texts, which belong at the end of the first century, clarify ideas about resurrection to the degree that they speak more definitely of resurrection and the relationship between body and soul. With the views represented in the following writings the transition to rabbinic literature takes place.

5. The Similitudes of Ethiopian Enoch

Whereas in the earlier parts of the Enoch tradition we found mainly statements about the fate of the souls or spirits of the righteous or the wicked, in the Similitudes the ideas about the resurrection become more concrete: 'In those days, Sheol will return all the deposits which she had received and hell will give back all that it owes' (I Enoch 51.1). The judgment takes place and the righteous will live on earth (51.1–5). The wicked do not take part in the resurrection: 'The faces of the strong will be slapped and be filled with shame and gloom. Their dwelling places and their beds will be worms. They shall have no hope to rise from their beds, for they do not extol the name of the Lord of the Spirits' (46.6).

6. The Liber Antiquitatum Biblicarum

In death the soul is separated from the body (44.10); the two also have different fates: the bodies of the disobedient people are destroyed, and the souls are imprisoned in 'dark chambers' (15.5; *thesauri* corresponds to *pronuptuaria* in IV Ezra, see there); the souls of the righteous are preserved (in chambers?) until the end-time (23.13). Alongside this tradition of the ongoing existence of souls is that of the general resurrection followed by the judgment and a glorious end-time on earth (3.10); here God is the one who acts: *Vivificabo mortuos et erigam dormientes de terra*: 'I will bring the dead to life and raise those who sleep from the earth' (3.10; cf. I Enoch 51.1, 'who brings the dead to life', see below, and Rom.4.17). Here the resurrection of the total person (body and soul) is expected (cf. also 19.12; 51.5), eternal life of the risen on a new earth. So in *Liber Antiquitatum Biblicarum* the two notions of the continuation of souls after death and the resurrection of the whole person stand unconnected side by side.

7. The IV Ezra Apocalypse

The two traditions of the resurrection and preservation of souls in chambers appear in the depiction of the end-events with the judgment of the world in IV Ezra 7.26–44:

*'Et terra reddet qui in eam dormiunt
et pulvis qui in eo silentio habitant,
et promptuaria reddent quae eis commendatae sunt animae'* (32).
'And the earth shall give up those who are asleep in it,
and the dust those who dwell in it in silence,
and the chambers shall give up the souls which have been
committed to them' (cf.4.41–42).

The juxtaposition of the two notions leads to the question: 'Where is the dead person before the resurrection, and how does one nevertheless have to imagine the resurrection?'[5] On the one hand the souls are in the chambers and are freed from them, and the body arises from earth and dust. However, 'The resurrection is not yet directly thought of as a reunion of body and soul, though this notion is already very near.'[6]

8. The Syrian Apocalypse of Baruch (SyrBar)

Of all the writings discussed so far, this work deals with the question of the resurrection body (cf.I Cor.15.35) in the most direct and concrete way (49–51). First of all the dead will arise in their original bodily form 'to show those who live that the dead are living again' (50.3); after that is the judgment. Then the guilty and the righteous will be changed, the wicked for the worse, and the righteous to angelic splendour (cf. I Enoch 51.4f.); in other words, first comes the resurrection into earthly corporeality, identical with the original, as a proof of the resurrection, and then the transformation. The life of those who have been changed into glory is not on the earth, even on a renewed earth, but 'the extents of Paradise will be spread out for them, and to them will be shown the majesty of the living beings under the throne, as well as all the hosts of angels' (51.11). Alongside this in the Syrian Apocalypse of Baruch there is also the idea of the preservation of the souls in chambers which will be opened at the end of the messianic time (30.5). So here too the traditions of the chambers for souls and the physical resurrection are combined.

Summary

The traditional biblical notion of ongoing life in Sheol was combined with the (Greek) notion of the immortality of the soul and had to be brought into harmony with the holistic anthropology of Israel. The texts presented bear witness to the struggle for clarity, which was not wholly successful.

III. The Qumran texts

The Qumran discoveries do not represent a unified corpus; a smaller proportion of the (non-biblical) writings arises out of the theological activity of the community. Despite the largely traditional character of the Qumran community it is striking that there are no clear statements about a resurrection of the dead in its own writings. The texts which are most discussed, 1QH 6.32–34; 11.12, cannot be interpreted in terms of an eschatological resurrection of the dead;[7] in 1QH 6.32–34 the conceptuality of death stands for lowliness, and 1QH 11.12 is in the context of present salvation and the community with the angels bestowed in that.[8]

These findings from statements about a future resurrection of the dead which are by no means clear can be interpreted in different ways: either the Qumran community has no hope of the future resurrection of the dead or it took it for granted to such a degree that it did not need to become a specific theme.

At all events, the method of burial in Qumran indicates that the pious counted on an event after death, so that while Josephus' report on the Essene belief in the 'immortality of souls' (Josephus, *War* 2, 154;

Antiquities 18.18) may be in Greek garb, it does speak aptly of a future hope.[9]

The questionability of evidence for the future resurrection remains a problem even in the face of newly published fragments which know a future resurrection (taking up Ezek.37), namely 4Q Second Ezekiel.[10] There is now clear evidence for the resurrection of the dead by the Messiah in 4Q521.12,[11] in the context of messianic expectations according to Isa.61.1 and taking up Isa.26.19.

IV. The rabbinic literature

Contrary to the conservative standpoint of the Sadducees who deny resurrection and judgment – since for them these cannot be derived from the Torah (Josephus, *War* 2, 165; *Antiquities* 18.16; Mark 12.18–27; Acts 4.1–2; 23.8) – it is constitutive of the Pharisaic rabbinic tradition that 'All Israel has a portion in the world to come: those who say that there is no making alive of the dead from the Torah' (mSanh 10.1). God is 'the One who brings the dead to life' (Second Benediction of the Eighteen Benedictions), and the morning prayer (bBer 60b) makes it clear (see the pictorial representation in Dura Europos) how this bringing to life is to be imagined: 'To you be praise, O Lord, who restore the souls to the dead bodies.' The place occupied by the resurrection in the morning prayer is connected with the notion that sleep is like death. In sleep the soul ascends to heaven and is reunited with the body in the morning.[12]

The discussion of mSanh 10.1 in bSanh 90a–92b concentrates on the questions whether the resurrection of the dead can be derived from the Torah (or scripture), how the resurrection body is to be envisaged and whether the resurrection is plausible at all ('Can the dust live?'). The problems to be clarified are those of identity between the former existence and resurrection existence and at the same time of responsibility. The parable of the lame and the blind is told in this context: body and soul have sinned together, are responsible together and will be punished together (91a-b);[13] the problems of physical identity are answered in the same kind of way as in the Syrian Apocalypse of Baruch: 'They will rise with their infirmities and be healed' (91b).

The question of the form of the resurrection is also put in the parable of the grain of wheat (cf. I Cor.15.36–38; John 12.24): 'If they rise again will they then be naked or rise in garments? He (R.Meir) replied to her (Cleopatra): Then a conclusion can be drawn from easier to more difficult by comparing a grain of wheat. If a grain of wheat which is buried naked arises with many garments, how much more so will the righteous, who are buried in their garments' (b.Sanh 90b; for the imagery orientated on vegetation see Isa.66.14; Ps.72.16).[14]

Identity is guaranteed on the one hand by 'the notion that something remains of the matter of the body and at the resurrection develops back into the full form of the dead person',[15] and on the other with the principle 'as one goes away, so he returns'; only after that are physical infirmities healed.

Burial in the land of Israel has a special significance: 'Anyone who is buried in the land of Israel is as it were buried under the altar' (bKet 111a); the ossuaries give evidence of this, since they often contain bones from the Diaspora which have been buried a second time.

The coming of the dead to resurrection in the land of Egypt is explained after 300 with the imagery of winding through subterranean caves and passages to the land of Israel (Gilgul); thus the Jews of the Diaspora also take part in the resurrection in the land of Israel.[16] This view represents an ancient holistic notion which is unimpressed by a dichotomistic separation of body and soul and sees a revival in the resurrection.

In the Kabbala Gilgul takes on the significance of the migration of souls: the soul can be reincarnated a thousand times and more, either for punishment (also in animals) or in the case of the righteous for the preservation of the world. In this notion the dichotomistic separation of body and soul is taken furthest, so that the problem of identity and thus of responsibility and punishment is posed anew.[17]

Translated by John Bowden

Select Bibliography

Biblical quotations are taken from the Revised Standard Version and quotations from intertestamental literature from James H. Charlesworth (ed.), *The Old Testament Pseudepigrapha* (2 vols.), New York and London 1983, 1985.

C. Barth, *Die Errettung vom Tode in den individuellen Klage- und Dankliedern des Alten Testaments*, Zurich 1947, new ed. by B. Janowski, Zurich 1987

P. Billerbeck, *Kommentar zum Neuen Testament aus Talmud und Midrasch* (4 vols.), Munich [6]1975

H. C. C. Cavallin, *Life after Death. Paul's Arguments for the Resurrection of the Dead in I Cor.15. Part I: An Enquiry into the Jewish Background*, Lund 1974

– , 'Leben nach dem Tode im Spätjudentum und in frühen Christentum', *Aufstieg und Niedergang der römischen Welt* II, 19.1, 240–345

M. Hengel, *Judaism and Hellenism* (two vols.), London and Philadelphia 1974

B. Janowski, *Rettungsgewissheit und Epiphanie des Heils. Das Motiv der Hilfe Gottes 'am Morgen' im Alten Orient und im Alten Testament, I, Alter Orient*, Neukirchen 1989

H. W. Kuhn, *Enderwartung und gegenwärtiges Heil. Untersuchungen zu den Gemeindeliedern in Qumran*, Göttingen 1966

H. Lichtenberger, *Studien zum Menschenbild in Texten der Qumrangemeinde*, Göttingen 1980

G. W. E. Nickelsburg, *Resurrection, Immortality and Eternal Life in Intertestamental Judaism*, London 1972

G. Scholem, *Encyclopaedia Judaica* 7, 573–7

– , *Von der mystischen Gestalt der Gottheit*, Zurich 1962

G. Stemberger, *Der Leib der Auferstehung*, Rome 1972

– , 'Das Problem der Auferstehung im Alten Testament', *Kairos* 14, 1972, 273–90

– , 'Zur Auferstehungslehre in der rabbinischen Literatur', *Kairos* 15, 1973, 238–66

– , 'Auferstehung I/2 Judentum', *TRE* 4, 443–50

– , *Studien zum rabbinischen Judentum*, Stuttgart 1990

E. E. Urbach, *The Sages, Their Concepts and Beliefs*, Jerusalem 1975

L. Wächter, *Der Tod im Alten Testament*, Berlin 1967

Notes

1. Cf. Wächter, *Tod im Alten Testament*, 181–98.

2. Hengel, *Judaism and Hellenism* I, 196–207.

3. For what follows see the monographs by Cavallin, Nickelsburg and Stemberger mentioned in the bibliography.

4. Hengel, *Judaism and Hellenism* I (n.2), 198.

5. Stemberger, *Leib*, 78.

6. Ibid., 84.

7. Lichtenberger, *Menschenbild*, 219–23.

8. Kuhn, *Enderwartung*, 78–93.

9. Lichtenberger, *Menschenbild*, 229–309.

10. J. Strugnell and D. Dimnant, *Revue de Qumrân* 13, 1988, 45–58; cf. E. Puech, ibid., 82.

11. M. O. Wise and J. D. Tabor, 'The Messiah at Qumran', *Biblical Archaeology Review* 18.6, 1992, 60–5.

12. Cf. Stemberger, 'Auferstehungslehre', 248f.

13. Ibid., 250–4.

14. Ibid., 239–47.

15. Ibid., 256.

16. Billerbeck III, 828,830; IV.2, 1198; Stemberger, 'Auferstehungslehre', 258–60.

17. Cf. Scholem, *Encyclopaedia Judaica* 7, 573–7; id., *Von der mystischen Gestalt der Gottheit*, 193–247.

Reincarnation and Modern Gnosis

David S. Toolan

Once for each thing. Just once; no more. And we too, just once. And never again.

(Rainer Maria Rilke, *Ninth Duino Elegy*)

We are living in what the Greeks called the *kairos* – the right moment – for a 'metamorphosis of the gods', of the fundamental principles and symbols.

(Carl Gustav Jung, *Collected Works*, 10, 585–6)

God's goodness, we read in Plato and St Bonaventure, is diffusive of itself. But sometimes it takes a stranger to defamiliarize the familiarity of this claim. In the summer of 1982, I attended a Christian-Buddhist dialogue at the Naropa Institute in Boulder, Colorado; and quite the most intriguing event of that week was an interview I had with Jamgon Kongtrul, a twenty-six-year-old Tibetan monk who in a previous lifetime, I was told, had been incarnate as a very wise nineteenth-century lama, a noted artist, scholar and ecumenist who had done much to reconcile Vajrayana Buddhism with the animistic folk religion of the peasantry. Since in this former incarnation he had merited release from the cycle of death and rebirth and attained nirvana, the affable young man sitting opposite me held the honorific of 'Tulku', which meant that he was a bodhisattva – someone who had been to heaven and freely elected to return to earth.

With a journalist's nose for the sensational, I tried to steer the conversation to the mechanics of metempsychosis, but Jamgon Kongtrul led me to the root of the matter. He spoke instead of compassion, the motive and meaning of his life, indeed, of his whole religious tradition. It seems that it wasn't enough to save one's own skin, that loving kindness could draw you back to work for the salvation of all sentient beings.

I hardly remember his exact words. What I cannot forget is what the man's presence conveyed – nothing less than goodness diffused, radiant. Sitting opposite me, in effect, was a living, breathing embodiment of self-emptying for others. In this young Tibetan monk, I found myself approaching something like the theophany of Sinai: 'I have indeed seen . . . I have heard . . . I have taken heed of their sufferings, and I have come down . . .' (Ex. 3. 7–8). Then, as the monk spoke of the evil of 'clinging' to anything, even to the highest mystical experience or heaven itself, I heard an echo of St Paul's hymn in Philippians 2.6: 'His state was divine, yet he did not cling to his equality with God but emptied himself.' It suddenly struck me: if we can't fathom Jamgon Kongtrul's sacrificial sense of reincarnation, then it's far-fetched to imagine we have understood anything at all in the meaning of the Incarnation!

I tell this story at the outset of these reflections on the current Western fascination with previous existence to counter the conventional presumption that belief in reincarnation always carried morally objectionable consequences, such as implying fatalism or an excuse for procrastination (as in St Augustine's 'Give me chastity but not yet'). Or that it is morally paralysing ('no use fighting my karma'). By habit, I think, Christians are inclined to construe the doctrine in these invidious ways, comparing it unfavourably with the tone of moral urgency given to a lifetime by the presumption that this is a one-chance affair not to be squandered. But clearly, if Jamgon Kongtrul is any example, multiplying the one chance of a lifetime by a factor of 10 or 100 does not mean that reincarnation cannot serve as an emblem of awesome charity, freedom and self-sacrifice. The key question is, what is the whole soteriological frame in which reincarnation finds its place? Depending on its larger interpretative context, reincarnation can be taken in several ways – as morally urgent, for instance, proclaiming as a bodhisattva does that 'nothing shall be lost', or conversely, as narcissistic self-inflation at the price of denigrating creation. The question I will discuss here is how the doctrine is being framed and understood within the context of North America in the 1990s. But first, some sociological facts.

I. The statistics

Confidence that the life-journey is, as the poet Rilke put it, a 'just once . . . never again' affair, would seem to have suffered considerable leakage in recent decades. The statistics can come as a shock. According to the most recent Eurobarometer survey I have seen (autumn 1989), 21% of Europeans believe in reincarnation. What is particularly striking, however, is the fact that about a third of regularly practising European Catholics (31%) and Protestants (37%) profess belief in reincarnation. The figures for the United States are comparable. According to a 1990 Gallup poll, almost one in four Americans (21%) subscribe to reincarnation, whereas 22% are not sure. (11% believe in clairvoyance, the power of the mind to know the past and predict the future; 25% take astrology seriously; and 11% think that 'spirit-beings' can temporarily assume control of a human being during a trance, i.e. 'channelling'.)

From these statistics, one can infer that when we speak of belief in the transmigration of the soul from one embodiment to another, we are not addressing a marginal phenomenon. This is not a belief confined to spiritualists, occultists or so-called New Age religiosity. On the contrary, the belief in past lives is being mainlined into a culture at large. The question is why. What is the meaning and appeal of this doctrine?

In the sections to follow, I will consider what reincarnation means and how it functions within two basic settings: New Age thinking and past life therapy. Very different consequences follow from each. Finally, I will consider the appeal of this doctrine to the wider public in the United States.

II. Recycling the harmonial tradition

Strictly speaking, researchers have only been able to locate some 26,000 Americans (mostly of the cosmopolitan left) who define themselves as New Age believers in a sense analogous to belonging to a church. But as a diffuse mood of spiritual adventurism, the New Age ethos is pervasive. The phenomenon has to be understood as arising out of the traumas of the 1960s and 1970s. Civil rights battles, political assassinations, Vietnam and Watergate, after all, had undermined our 'civil religion' – that amalgam of biblical tradition and republican virtue that up until then had held the national psyche together. The result was a spiritual vacuum – into which rushed Eastern gurus and all those who claimed to be bearers of hidden wisdom passed on to them from contemporary representatives of ancient pre- and non-Christian 'mystery schools'. Early Christian Gnosticism and the theosophy of Helena Petrovna Blavatsky and her various offspring gained a new foothold, as did the millenarian visions of Joachim of Fiore (and Teilhard de Chardin). Room was also found for the ritual magic of the Eliphas Levi school, with origins (real and alleged) in ancient shamanism, the Knights Templar, thirteenth-century Kabbalism, the secret wisdom of the Tarot, and so forth. Anything 'established' was the enemy.

People underestimate how receptive American soil is to such syncretistic, antinomian experimentation. For two centuries now, ever since
Ralph Waldo Emerson (1803–82) railed against the established Calvinist
churches and first evoked it in his famous Divinity School Address of 1836,
something very like either Hindu pantheism or Bonaventure's emanation-
ism (take your pick) has run in the American blood. The world, Emerson
had declared, 'is not the product of manifold power, but of one will, of one
mind; and that one mind is everywhere active, in each ray of the star, in
each wavelet of the pool . . . All things proceed out of the same spirit, and
all things conspire with it.' Hence, nothing is profane; the Sage of
Concord, as it was said, saw sermons 'not just in stones but in bean rows at
Walden Pond and mud puddles in Boston Common'. Hence also 'the
mystery of the soul', 'the greatness of man'. 'One man [Jesus],' Emerson
asserted, 'was true to what is in you and me. He saw that God incarnates
himself in man, and ever more goes forth anew to take possession of his
world. He said . . . "I am divine. Through me, God acts; through me,
speaks. Would you see God, see me; or see thee, when thou also thinkest as
I now think."'

Question: Is this Bonaventure and Meister Eckhart? Or is it an expositor
of Advaita Vedanta (Shamkara perhaps), or a Gnostic Christian identifying the 'seed of light' at the core of the human soul with God – and
proposing a flight from materiality and history? The point is that
Americans have taken Emersonian 'self-reliance', which at root means
God-reliance, in all these directions. Moreover, starting in the 1830s and
ever mindful of how corrupt all established churches are (i.e., giving us a
suffering, crucified Jesus rather than a purely resurrected one), highly
mobile Americans have repeatedly set out on the romantic quest to
discover what Emerson heralded: the secret abyss of inwardness, that self-
within-a-self which utterly antecedes and transcends the fallen, created
world. And new religious movements are the time-tested way we set about
this task. Nothing runs in the American grain so much as starting over to
rediscover innocence, Adam and Eve responding to the breeze of God in
the Garden. America, Emerson said, 'has no past: all has an onward and
prospective look'.

Emerson is the American Schleiermacher; he personifies ecstatic New
World energy, without which history is cut off from inspiration and new
meaning, without which it goes dead, merely repeats, slides into entropy.
He is our archetypal *puer aeternus* (eternal youth), full of that mercurial
eros that would later inspire Walt Whitman's magical act of remaining 'me
myself' while simultaneously merging with every crowd. As the

enthusiastic oracle of the 'God in you that responds to the God without' – a kind of realized eschatology – Emerson spoke to everyman's subjunctive mood – of all our might bes, may bes, and what ifs – as people of direct access to the spirit will. And the New Age, with its upbeat rhetoric and serene synthesizer meditation music (sounding more like Jean Jacques Rousseau), tries to follow suit. The mystical pedigree here ('the alone to the Alone') is excellent, descending from Plato, Plotinus, Scotus Erigena, Meister Eckhart, Jacob Boehme, Spinoza and Madam Guyon. Emerson democratized them, made the cosmic connection available to the public (no elitism here!) – unfortunately at too low a price. He forgot to mention what Eckhart and Pantanjali knew: the necessity of fulfilling certain conditions – like making oneself pure of heart and poor of spirit.

Thus, as Emerson's Transcendentalism passed into other hands, it became a parody, a case of 'cheap grace' eclipsing nature, and banked for its 'cash value' and hygienic possibilities. Emerson's 'self-reliance' was transformed into what the historian Sidney E. Ahlstrom calls the 'harmonial tradition', the central axiom of which is that 'spiritual composure, physical health, and even economic well-being are understood to flow from a person's rapport with the cosmos.'[1] By the turn of the century, in so-called New Thought, God had metamorphosed into 'the divine supply', an unfailing gas depot for entrepreneurs on the fast track. (The California Hinduism of actress Shirley MacLaine had plenty of precedent.)

The problem of harmonial tradition is not philistinism, 'tranquillizing oneself with the trivial' as Kierkegaard would have put it, but the sickness unto death of 'too much possibility'. That defect, I think, is clear when you examine Emerson's vulgarizing successors: Mary Baker Eddy's mind-curing Christian Science, the 'esoteric Christianity' of utilitarian New Thought at the turn of the century, and the denial-based 'positive thinking' of Ralph Waldo Trine and Norman Vincent Peale in this century. In all these inflections of harmonial thought, Emerson's flaws are flagrant: a mysticism that occurs in isolation, that puts the self against the community, and turns true believers into bad citizens who are almost constitutionally incapable of assuming responsibility for social institutions – or changing them.

Being for the most part anti-intellectual, ahistorical and pragmatic, New Agers are not likely to acknowledge the foregoing as their lineage. (They want 'workshops', not lectures.) Nor, bewitched by all their positive thinking and self-affirmations, are they likely to credit that the mystical idealism and freedom which they espouse – it's so beautiful! – sometimes conceals a dark, Gnostic aversion for the created world, a kind of despair over material nature and society. Instead, they see themselves as the vanguard of new Copernican revolutions, new paradigm shifts, in medicine, psychology, science, politics, business and education. Their rhetoric is ascensional, an ultrasupernaturalism that eclipses nature and denies history. We are not limited by conditions or conditioning, they proclaim, we are the future being born. But to make the self coeval with God, as they often do, is equivalently to seek freedom from the world, from time, and from other selves. Implicitly, creation is envisioned, as the early Gnostics saw it, as a catastrophe, something from which one's divine 'spark' must seek escape. The question to ask the New Age globalists (at the risk of fatally clipping their wings) is whether or not they are in flight from history.

Which is not to say that New Age enthusiasm is inauthentic. The world's ruling cliques, its Amfortases – overburdened, wounded and hard of heart – cannot do without such creative energy. Else, nothing is left but law and order. At the same time, when enthusiasm is split off from the archetypal energy of the wise and crafty old king/queen in us, the danger is easily seen. Too often, New Agers are Icarus on the way to the sun, Phaethon driving the sun's chariot out of control, Bellerophon ascending on bright winged Pegasus – only to fall, crash. Because of a certain grandiosity and inability to accept limits – or what Nathaniel Hawthorne would have called an 'angelic imagination' that escapes into the future rather than face the complexity of the present – the movement lacks sobriety, substance and sagacity. The paradox is that enthusiasts must fall from innocence to acquire the weighty conscience of an adult.

So much, then, for the frame of New Age notions of reincarnation and its major performance art, the idea of serving as mouthpiece for various disincarnate spirits of 'ascended masters'. The psychic transmission business would prove highly profitable.

III. New Age channelling

The function of reincarnation and the law of karma – that we reap what we sow – within the forthrightly Pelagian context of contemporary New Age thinking and packaging remains highly problematic. Indeed, the legacy of 'positive thinking' is poisonous. The handiest evidence for this judgment is provided by channelling or mediumship – whereby individuals in a state of trance transmit the putative wisdom of the 'other world'. In recent decades, through the 'Seth' books of Jane Roberts, Helen Cohn

Schucman's 'Course in Miracles', Kevin Ryerson's readings, and J. Z. Knight's 35,000 year-old 'Ramtha', mediumship has once again become a major industry catering to the spiritually hungry.

To illustrate, let me cite Jack Pursel, a former insurance agent from Michigan who is better known under the name of 'Lazaris', the 'ascendant master' whom Pursel psychically mediates before thousands in seminars throughout the country (a four-day intensive costs $600).[2] Pursel/Lazaris is consulted by Hollywood stars, by doctors and lawyers, stock analysts and a few bank directors for advice on marital matters, menstrual problems and how to make money; and through a promotion company called Concept:Synergy, he markets a 32-page catalogue of audiotapes, videotapes and books. The basic message (delivered in a Scottish brogue) is pop psychology: to break the 'dark Law' of childhood belief that life will be painful and tragic instead of successful, happy and content. When the client's problem does not seem grounded in the present life, Lazaris nonchalantly locates the difficulty in a previous life.

The climax of a Lazaris seminar consists of a meditation that promises to plug participants into the transforming power of Sirius, the brightest star in our hemisphere. Sirius energy, it is claimed, offers the key to happiness, which is defined as self-determination or 'creating your own reality'. New Age spiritual efforts, Lazaris assures his audiences, created the reality of the demonstrations in Eastern Europe and South Africa that, respectively, overthrew Communism and apartheid.

Now no Catholic who grew up with guardian angels or who takes the Hebrew prophets seriously will have trouble with the concept of channelling itself. The Bible is full of it. The problem is the revelation here: that it sounds like the word of a twice-born Ronald Reagan, for whom religious experience is strictly for private consumption without redeeming social purpose. The Lazaris message goes down smoothly with a well-heeled audience, many of whom are already too 'liberated' from family and social history. As understandably it should – because as creating one's own reality is understood in this narcissistic context, it implies that the hungry, sick and destitute have chosen their reality (i.e., refused Sirius energy), just as the wealthy, successful, beautiful and talented have chosen theirs. The implication is clear: Third World countries suffer dreadful conditions because the people there are spiritual refusniks. The unfortunate have only themselves to blame; whereas First World affluence indicates moral superiority, is a sign of election. (Where have we Calvinist Americans heard this before?) The *laissez-faire* individualist, so exalted during the recent Ronald Reagan and Margaret Thatcher era, can go away absolved, his or her conscience soothed with a Good Housekeeping seal of approval. If there were ever a case of spirituality as an opiate, this surely must qualify.

The message of J. Z. Knight's 'Ramtha' (popularized by actress Shirley Maclaine's best selling books) is similarly soporific. Helen Cohn Schucman's 'Course in Miracles' has a decidedly Gnostic ring, but is in some ways saved by its stress on the virtues of forgiveness and charity. With this one exception, however, what is remarkable is the uniformly narcissistic message of the channellers – and the impression that all their astral beings went to the Harvard Business School.

IV. Past Life Therapy

If New Age channelling gives reincarnation a bad name, its growing use in 'past life therapy' provides a more complex and better grounded story – thanks, I think, to its links to a Freudian earthiness. Catharsis and ecstasy there is, but only *after* undergoing a dark night of soul. And that harrowing of soul casts a very different light on the truism that each of us is responsible for our own reality. Clearly, we do co-operate in constructing our own prisons and gardens of Eden, and do, collectively, make a world of 'fact' that in turn shapes and misshapes our psyches. (Like St Augustine's profound aphorism, 'Love and do what you will,' however, creating one's own reality is a notion subject to grave misunderstanding.)

Characteristically, the therapeutic approach to reincarnation places primary emphasis on the subjective experience of the client and leaves questions of historical and metaphysical truth in suspension. To the psychotherapist, the issue is whether reminiscences of this sort, usually induced by hypnosis or trance, bring relief from painful symptoms and destructive behaviour. The client's reports need not be taken literally, only seriously.

Of the dozens of books by past life therapists currently on the stand, Jungian analyst Roger J. Woolger's *Other Lives, Other Selves*[3] is probably the most sophisticated. Consider one of his patients, a fifty-year-old osteopath with the pseudonym 'Sol', who sought therapy after a visit to the Wailing Wall in Jerusalem, where he found himself weeping uncontrollably. Though meticulous about his health, Sol has suffered all his life from incurable sinusitus. When he tries, under a light trance, to recall when the condition originated, he remembers himself cold and wet in summer camp at the age of nine, feeling that he will never again see his dying mother. Woolger begins to suspect that Sol is still stoically holding that grief in his sinuses, and asks Sol to repeat the phrase, 'I'll never see her again' – and see where it takes him. The phrase gradually changes to 'I'll never see *him* again' – and suddenly Sol leapfrogs back to Palestine of the first century.

Sobbing and speaking in the voice of an alter ego, Sol says, 'They've taken him. I'll never see him again! What am I going to do? We could have done something. It's too late. We abandoned him. I'm standing behind a large crowd. It's Jerusalem. I'm a man in a long robe. They've taken Jesus. I'll never see him again. I'll never see him again!'[4]

Sol reports that from a distance, he watches Jesus being dragged to his death and crucified with common thieves. He, Sol, understands himself to have been a Roman commercial traveller who had come to Jerusalem on business, witnessed Jesus healing and become a disciple, eventually dying in his bed in old age among other Christians. Dr Woolger, the therapist, is indifferent to the issue of historical veracity; what concerns him is Sol's sense of abandonment and loss – and the cathartic memory that both relieves the man's chronic sinus condition and gives a burst of new meaning to Sol's healing work as an osteopath.

Few of the past life memories that Woolger reports are so uplifting or quickly resolved. His clients come to him suffering from chronic somatic symptoms, depression, irrational phobias, martyr complexes, sexual difficulties, eating disorders and family struggles. And typically, they don't remember themselves as glamorous Nefertiti or Rameses II but rather as abused peasants, prostitutes, tyrants, bandits, slaves or victims of rape and mayhem. What Woolger and other therapists like him probe is the longer story of woundedness behind the current story, the unfinished drama of the soul – and often that larger story seems buried deep in the tissue, far behind the childhood and birth traumas where Freud or Otto Rank would have located it. Unlike the quick-fix aspirin of the New Age psychics, working through the thralldoms of past life stories typically forces the client to face a dark psychic inheritance that has all the marks of Original Sin.

What is particularly striking is the frequency with which inherited impairments condense around experiences of dying – as if people are subconsciously programmed for a following lifetime by their last thoughts before death. Thoughts of repentance – 'I was selfish; I need to care about others' can seemingly catapult a person into a subsequent life as a nun in a leper colony. Whereas bitter thoughts seem to drag one down. And the work of detaching from these deeply set thought complexes is not ego-inflating. The client has to sit with his or her opposites and endure the conflict. For in tracking the unfolding of a complex through several lifetimes, polar opposites often appear: the client is both Cain and Abel, Iphegenia and Medea, Prometheus and Narcissus, Sarah and Hagar, Jekyll and Hyde. Facing up to the shadow side of oneself, says Woolger, is the way to exorcise it. And here, he claims, an experience of death and afterlife becomes critical. For once the person has wholly identified with some conflicted sub-personality from a prior lifetime, an experience of the transition state between death and rebirth allows the client freely to detach from the now manifest destructive complex. In short, experiencing a former after-life gives one psychological distance, and thus leverage. It means the freedom to decide between good and evil.

An example would be 'Madeleine',[5] a young teacher who came to Woolger in a state of near-suicidal depression. Over many sessions, doctor and client discover a series of past lives in which violent deaths, torture and rape recur repeatedly with the dominant thought 'It's all my fault. I am a wicked person and deserve to suffer'. It's a cycle of self-induced martyrdom or karmic expiation that seems to go nowhere. In time, however, Madeleine remembers herself, in gory detail, in a quite opposite role – as a barbaric pirate who brutalizes his victims mercilessly. Eventually alone and destitute in a tavern, the pirate/Madeleine dies – and then moves into a timeless zone between death and rebirth. The pirate finds himself in an outer darkness on a remote, abandoned planet, where he wanders as a ghost, seemingly for ever – in punishment. 'I'm punishing myself,' the pirate/Madeleine says. '[T]his is what I have to do to atone for what I have done to others and in order to be human again I have to feel what my victims must have felt before they died, desolate, alone and without hope.' In subsequent sessions, Madeleine revisits all the faces of the men, women and children she had murdered as a pirate – in what Woolger calls an 'extraordinary act of contrition'. Eventually, however, she hears a graceful, forgiving voice saying: 'Enough, enough. You have done enough.'

Woolger's privileged clients are not retracing their steps into the past in order to evade present reality. The source of Madeleine's inexplicable depression was not her parents (as Freudian theory might suppose), but, presumably, the conflict within her between the stories of the brutal pirate and the multitude of (atoning) victims that, unwittingly, she carried into her present life. Whatever one makes of her vivid recollections – whether they are products of a collective unconscious or actual memories of individual past lifetimes – the whole point of the therapy is to support her as she confronts and gains release from these inner horror stories of a master-slave complex – so that they no longer unconsciously predetermine her life. Moreover, according to Woolger, by learning to know and understand the dreadful cast of inner characters that inhabit one's unconscious, many of them of the opposite sex and from foreign cultures, his clients learn tolerance and compassion. They typically come away with distinct feelings of solidarity and empathetic identity with other cultures and peoples who suffer in far-off parts of the world at present. In this therapeutic context, then, reincarnation does not function as a narcotic; nor does it promote the dissociated sensibility celebrated by New Age psychopomps.

V. The wider appeal of reincarnation

Short of unusual psychic experience like the above, the power and plausibility of the idea of reincarnation arises for others, Christians among them, from the same locus in experience as do the calls, in justice, for 'equal opportunity', or, failing that, for a second chance and a new beginning. That is, it is a question of theodicy. The idea issues from experiences of misfortune or apparent injustice at either birth or death. Life's favours are distributed unfairly. Moreover, in affluent, technological countries where more is expected of life than was true of our preindustrial ancestors, the arbitrariness of birth and death are felt all the more acutely. Due to genetic defect or circumstance beyond the individual's control, some lives seem fated to utter misery. (Of starving Somali children or those born with AIDS or fetal alcohol syndrome, we find ourselves spontaneously saying, 'They never had a chance'.) Whereas other lives full of promise are suddenly cut short. And at the moment of death, still other lives appear arrested in mediocrity, neither virtuous enough for heaven nor so reprobate as to deserve damnation. It is cases of latter kind, of course, that once impelled twelfth-century theologians to postulate an intermediate realm between heaven and hell called purgatory – which functions in the Christian world-view the way reincarnation does in the Orient. The difference, of course, is that the Orient places purgatory on earth.

With infinite variation, then, what jams in the throat in all such cases as the above is a sense of incompletion or unfinishedness. And this feeling of incompletion is rendered all the sharper if one projects life in terms of a noble religious ideal. Indeed, purely secular conceptions of the good life may rest content with mediocrity or philistinism, but lofty religious norms such as the call to sanctity in Christianity or Buddhism demand more of life – and call out all the more insistently for second chances. In such contexts, what is really amazing is not that reincarnation would be thought a reasonable and consoling hypothesis, but that one could imagine completing the human project within the space of a single lifetime.

Secondly, Christians and others turn to the law of karma in revulsion at the morbid and literalistic way in which the Christian doctrine of the 'four last things' – death, judgment, hell and heaven – have been preached. For too long, the Western church overdid the motive of fear, inflating the terrors of death, making dire threats of ill-made confessions and communions, emphasizing the macabre tortures of the afterlife and picturing the God of mercy and love as a terrible judge whose function it was to sentence people to everlasting, excruciating punishment. It must be considered, writes the historian Jean Delumeau in his magisterial *Sin and Fear*, 'whether the rejection of an oppressive doctrinal campaign was one of the causes of the "de-Christianization" of the West'. 'No civilization,' he continues, 'had ever attached as much importance to guilt and shame as did the Western world from the thirteenth to the eighteenth centuries.'[6] In effect, argues Delumeau, the normal preaching of the church, both Catholic and Protestant, lost the balance of St Paul's dictum in Romans 5.20, effectively reversing it to read 'Where grace abounded, sin did more abound.'

Is it any wonder, then, that starting in the nineteenth century, Westerners began turning to oriental ideas that seemed to inculcate a more positive attitude toward the self as a 'spark of God', that gave evolutionary meaning to their moral struggles, and above all, that delivered them from anxiety before a seemingly captious divine judgment? True, doctrines of reincarnation and karma can be, and often enough are, construed in a pantheistic, Gnostic or Pelagian direction. But they need not be so interpreted. The great attraction of the law of karma, I think, lies in the fact that it is impersonal, that it does not minimize the terrible psychic inheritance many have to endure, and that at the same time it places full responsibility for the outcome of a life upon the individual's free (though often mistaken) choices. In addition, reincarnation provides one with a perspective on those troublesome triumphs of evil in the world, allowing us to see them as mere episodes in a much longer story in which justice will eventually prevail.[7]

VI. Final Reflections on karma

If there is truth to the supposition that some of us are 'old souls', then I would guess that amnesia about past lives is a good thing, a grace; it grants us the saving illusion of a clean slate for new learning – or unlearning. Depending on the context, however, a doctrine of reincarnation can have very different consequences, as we have seen. As it is deployed within the harmonial tradition and in most New Age channelling situations, it would appear only to reinforce a sense of rootlessness and vagrancy that all too many Americans bring with them – and depart with undeterred. Within the context of therapy, on the other hand, it might have precisely the opposite effect, reconnecting the person across time, race and culture to the burdens and promises of the past, awakening one to the urgency of the present, and perhaps giving new life to the whole set of traditional religious ideas about birth, death and the after-life that previously made little sense. The one grave weakness of the therapeutic perspective, of course, lies in its introspective and individual focus, which may do little to enlighten the client on how insufficient a solitary liberation remains. That is to say, psychotherapy rarely facilitates insight into the communal dimension of redemption, nor does it highlight how social structures are implicated in individual pathologies. Though nothing is impossible with God, therapy by itself rarely awakens a sleeping bodhisattva.

Yet the irony of the current situation should not be lost. Millions, many of them unchurched, assume they are blessed or cursed with good or bad karma, temperamental orientations that they have to work with or 'work through' and shed – or face judgment at death. In effect, people are toying with a notion that suggests that both the cardinal virtues and the seven deadly sins may be more deeply rooted in the human psyche than childhood trauma or Oedipal struggles would warrant them to believe. To be sure, the karmic legacy may be promising; it can also be as grim and forbidding as anything that St Augustine imagined in his most brooding hours. Properly understood, the law of karma should be read as another way of talking about both original sin and merit – a psychic inheritance paralleling our genetic programme that, though it may in one case constitute a moral advantage, in another may just as well mean bondage of the mind and will to patterns set in ages past and all but incorrigible. Reincarnation thus belongs in the arsenal of those who take the mystery of evil seriously.

The curious thing is that this idea flourishes at precisely a time, after the Second Vatican Council, when Catholic preachers fall silent about 'sin' and the old concrete images of judgment, hell, purgatory and heaven. Revisionist theologians, apparently, find these images of the 'four last things' somewhat embarrassing, at best highly speculative, and emphasize instead the promised reign of God as it translates into a practical, vital hope for the here and now. The irony is that what we abandon, others take up. For while theologians attend to the urgent problems of changing social structures, hordes of sophisticated Westerners remain obsessed by the fear of death – and to allay it they have been getting what purport to be first-hand reports of the afterlife from psychics, the case histories of past life therapy, and *The Tibetan Book of the Dead*. None of this, they claim, is speculative. Ironically, it is from such testimonial sources, I suggest, that many feel the moral pressure to 'complete the race' in a single lifetime – if they can. The thought of having to repeat a lifetime again and again until one's lesson is learned serves as a goad to make every moment count – as if it were a grace.

Notes

1. Sydney E. Ahlstrom, *A Religious History of the American People*, New Haven 1972, 1019; cf. 1019–54, 600–6.

2. Cf. Michael D'Antonio, *Heaven on Earth: Dispatches from America's Spiritual Frontier*, New York 1992, 108–57.

3. Roger J. Woolger, *Other Lives, Other Selves: A Jungian Psychotherapist Discovers Past Lives*, New York 1988.

4. Ibid, 129; cf. also 127–37.

5. Ibid, 298–300; cf. also 280–306.

6. Jean Delumeau, *Sin and Fear: The Emergence of a Western Guilt Culture Thirteenth-Eighteenth Centuries*, New York, 1990, 557, 3, et passim.

7. Cf. Geddes MacGregor, *Reincarnation in Christianity: A New Vision of the Role of Rebirth in Christian Thought*, Wheaton, Ill. 1978, 1–26, 76–87, 99–116, 159–73.

Belief in Reincarnation in Africa

Jan Heijke

It is impossible to be too careful when making generalizations about Africa and Africans. There are common features, but also important differences, between the many ethnic groups on the continent. Thus ancestor worship is an ingredient of the African view of life from coast to coast.[1] Belief in reincarnation is much less a matter of course. According to the Nigerian author E. Bolaji Idowu, there is no reincarnation in the classical sense of the word in the African view of life.[2] The French anthropologist R. Jaulin agrees.[3] It is true that the notion of reincarnation can be found among the Urhobo of Nigeria, as another chance. The dead who are well established in the hereafter (Erivbin) prefer to continue as part of the ancestor group. But those who are not yet qualified for that ancestor-life are reincarnated, to improve their chances.[4] Even the very old are advised to reincarnate in order to make further progress. In Zimbabwe death, with the associated notion of reincarnation, offers the possibility of being reincarnated in the other sex, so that a new experience is possible.

However, it is not only *ethnic* differences which make it difficult to depict *the* African belief in reincarnation with broad brush-strokes. When one presents a panorama, the question which constantly recurs is whether it is a good thing to rely on qualified ethnological and cultural-anthropological studies, or whether it is better to use as a basis soundings among the youth in the cities of today, among teachers, market women, itinerant workers, farmworkers, fishermen, herdsmen, hunters, nomads, midwives, and so on. Anyone who wants to talk about Africa in a discussion about reincarnation must begin by pointing out a basic conviction which is closely connected with this subject. All kinds of statements and reactions by Africans, recorded by whites and blacks, indicate a concept of the *person* which differs from that of the average European. These witnesses indicate that Africans do not see and experience themselves as an undivided unity. They are convinced that they are composites. They are not in possession of themselves. The predominant sense – as far as it is reconstructed – is that human beings are made up of several components. The idea of being to a significant degree *derived* dominates behaviour. There is something, a segment in the person, which comes from *elsewhere*, from others.[5]

Westerners, on the other hand, are defined by *contrast* with others. The individual is a self, original. The individual's natural starting-point is the unalienable possession of his or her own identity. The African perspective does not know the division between self and other to this degree. On the contrary, the identity of the black person is never limited to 'that is not the other nor comes from the other'. Do such people not bear their own progenitors, their own ancestors, within themselves? For the African, 'I' is first of all social, and individual only after that. The African's starting point is, rather, the constant reception of the other. Also for Africans, the human person is not a closed system which sets itself over against the outside world. On the contrary, Africans try as far as possible to introduce themselves into the 'ambient sphere'[6] which permeates them in their turn. There is thus an osmosis which puts people in a position to listen to the pulse of the world.

From an African perspective, the Western man or woman is an 'orphan', a solitary figure without father or mother, who has to shape his or her own identity unaided. The Westerner seems able to give a very good answer to the question 'Who am I?' Such a person is limited, unique. Westerners see themselves as starting points, standing as it were in starting blocks. They are more successful, the more lines go out from them in the direction of the future.

By contrast, Africans would see themselves first of all as points of convergence in which all kinds of pre-natal lines come together. They define themselves first of all as recipients, as those who have been equipped. Many have contributed to them. They encounter the world around them as a place which has been prepared and made ready. The world has already been named, reconnoitred, subdivided, reclaimed, to a degree annexed. The contributions of others, of the generations which preceded them, are not fortuitous, but form an essential part of their identity. So for Africans the limits of the person are fluid, not fixed. Behind them – i.e. in the direction of the past – there stretches a very important substratum of their being. But in the opposite direction, too, in the direction of the future, they do not possess themselves. According to the African insight human beings do not have the same status from cradle to grave. The newborn gradually attain their humanity by being more and more integrated into previous, already existing society. In particular their status includes the task of 'prolongation', of producing 'offshoots'. The stream of life must not be blocked. Those who opt out of procreation put themselves outside society. The barren are primarily the unfortunate, the unfulfilled. Married couples who become parents take their place in the continuity, construct the social and biological web of which they form a part.

In short, Africans are borne along. They are carried forward by the living past. They constantly remember those who produced them. They remain as it were deeply under the impact of the world which others have prepared for their coming. They regard anything that they can add as being of lesser significance than that to which they are indebted. Is this an idyllic, romanticized picture? It is as idyllic as Christianity's Sermon on the Mount and the Buddhist interpretation of detachment for the Singhalese of Sri Lanka.

Anthropological studies show that Africans feel that the human person consists of a variety of components. The link between the various 'ingredients' is elastic – fragile, if you like. No matter what prople call the different elements or how they distinguish them, the view prevails that human beings do not completely control themselves, that the 'I' is brittle, that it possesses and can be possessed, that one can look at it in a detached way. By night a component of the person can begin to lead its own life, break out, escape from the grip of the 'I', but also be overcome by evil forces from outside. If they are not guided by another human being, these forces can have designs on one, drag one down, undermine one, sap one's strength, hound one's ego. The great importance attached to dreams illustrates this conviction about the composite nature of the person. The excursions made by the sleeping person show what limited control one has over oneself. Several persons dwell in one human being, and as a result of this the idea 'I' is relativized, dispossessed. The boundary with the other is removed; the 'I' is no longer even at home in itself; the alien is part of its constitution.[7]

Alongside the emphasis on the fragile character of the 'I' stands the conviction that an invulnerable, immortal component is part of the human person. The *sibbe* survives, and shows itself again in every new child. The principle of life, with its own distinct description, which is manifested in everyone who is born and which is received from predecessors, is not annihilated by death, but time and again shows itself in descendants. The biological chain is not an exclusive discovery of Africans. People every-where are preoccupied with things like heredity. What is characteristic of Africans is the importance that they attach to the ongoing line of generations. There is a constant that cannot be overwhelmed by death, something that is not purely biological or somatic, but has character and identity, and displays the family characteristics in which subsequent individuals share, from which they live. That social web plays an important role in the thought and action of Africans. They attribute a kind of independence to that family continuum which makes the loss of individual members easier to bear. For the family, death as it were does not exist, though it exists for the individual. As far as the family as a whole is concerned, the individual is of secondary importance.[8]

In Africa, reincarnation stands in the context of the family com-munity. For example, a mother can box her daughter's ears and be told by a bystander, 'You must not strike her, she is my mother.'[9] What can these words mean in the perception of the speaker and bystanders if not that a dead person has returned in a child? What relationship with the dead person is attributed to the child? There is certainly agreement that where the idea of reincarnation is found in Africa it functions as an emphasis on the continuity of the group. The Kikuyu of Kenya say that only the 'collective soul' – the group component – is reincarnated. The other 'soul' joins the ancestors. According to the Ashanti a component of the dead person returns to the ancestors and another component to God, and yet another component goes in the direction of those who have a close relationship.[10] 'Something' of the ancestor is thus thought to return, in a new individual. So this is partial rebirth. Most people think that the ancestor remains 'himself' where he was: in the 'king-dom of the dead'. The descendant is a composite 'other', a newcomer.[11]

In almost all cases the incarnated dead person seems to be a member of the family in the rising line of the same sex as the child, but never its own father or mother. Perhaps it may be a grandfather or grandmother.[12] Only those who have recently died are thought to be reincarnated in their grandchildren. More distant ancestors are (have become) anonymous and fall outside the expectation of reincarnation. Reincarnation of a dead person in a perfect stranger is ruled out.[13] So reincarnation puts people around the break between generations: where death interrupts the life shared by the group. The newborn is by the nature of things younger than the old person whose representative he is. Reincarnation in the strict sense should be identical repetition. Moreover the ancestor does not live on among his descendants in an integral or a highly personal way, as though under a pseudonym.

It is also significant that in Africa the notion of reincarnation seems to be concentrated on the first year of a child's life. An excursion to a local society, in this case a Senegalese village, may perhaps clarify this.[14] Experience teaches that a child is in danger the first week after birth, and may not come out of the hut. If the baby keeps crying, has green diarrhoea or eye problems, the mother goes to ask advice from an authorized 'donneur de nom', a soothsaying 'name-giver'. This person can say whether the problems indicated mean that an ancestor is trying to come back, under a particular name.

The diagnosis by which the 'knocking' of the ancestor is deciphered consists of an attentive study of the face of the baby, above all the wrinkles on its forehead. Sometimes lines on hands and feet are inspected.[15] The comparison then is not with the ancestor as an adult but as a baby who has just left its mother's womb. So the seer must have known the dead person well. Moreover the seer (who can be male or female) must remember the right (preferred) name of the dead person. If the seers make a mistake here, then the child is not healed. Consequently they usually restrict themselves to the treatment of the usual childhood illnesses from which most children recover. Hence, too, almost all children are reincarnations of ancestors. Only when the child is seven or eight years old does it get the name of 'its' ancestor. But then too (at the same time) the bond with the incarnated person begins to wear out.

A dead person can also be reincarnated several times: men up to four times, women to a maximum of three, according to some groups.[16] Here certain criteria seem to be taken into account. An ancestor can only reincarnate a second time if the host child is weaned and can walk. A 'name–giver' must not make a mistake here: it would be fatal for the potential second host child. In *successive* incarnations of the same ancestors the children share certain personal components among themselves. Simultaneous reincarnation is unknown. Furthermore, successive reincarnations can only take place within a limited period. When the bones of the ancestor perish there is no longer any question of reincarnation. Once the host children have grown up and eventually die themselves, they in turn can claim new life. So the genius of the family does not die but manifests itself in an unbroken line through descendants.

It goes without saying that anyone who has no children cannot reincarnate. Similarly, a-social individuals are excluded (according to the local criterion).

That reincarnation is thought to be life-preserving is confirmed by the interpretation given when a woman has a number of babies in succession which die young. In some societies these 'born-to-die' children are seen as the reincarnation of one and the same restless dead who nestles in a womb in order to be born and shortly afterwards to die again. Sometimes the baby is marked to provide a way of checking whether it returns after its death.

From what has been said we can conclude that reincarnation has a temporal character: that of a protecting 'indwelling'. That is to say that according to the African view, reincarnation is situated on the break between the generations, and moreover seems to be limited to the vulnerable period. When the period which is statistically dangerous has passed, then the indwelling stops. The component attributed to the ancestor is a continuity factor which is thought to steer the young child safely through the threatened first phase of life. The ancestor helps the child as it were to go through this phase.[17]

However, the ancestor is more than a guardian patron: in some way he himself comes to life again in the child. According to the Serer, originally a hunting people with a very developed sense of smell, the child has the physical odour – a mark of identity – of the ancestor of whom it is the reincarnation. But the physical odour is fleeting and gradually disappears after birth. So the ancestor-prothesis opens up the way for what is new, what has not yet been shown, for the surprising. That is why no one refers to a previous life.

Most Africans are convinced that each individual is in some sense reincarnated. To put it loosely: no one is his own origin. Westerners would also affirm that after some reflection. However, for Africans the bond with those who have opened up the world for them is so impressive that they want to keep the sense of it alive by means of an institution: ancestor worship. This formalized recollection of those who prepared the world for their descendants guarantees the respect for all kinds of rules and instructions and must prevent freebooting and individualism. Here we are entering new ground which goes outside the framework of this article.

Two last remarks. In the whole process of the succession of generations many groups in Africa also recognize something transcendent. Lured by the physical odour which the ancestor communicates to the descendant, as his most distinctive feature, *God* gives each individual a most distinctive, an unalienable component, according to the Senegalese village dwellers mentioned earlier. Secondly, it cannot be ruled out that as infant mortality is reduced, so belief in reincarnation will decline. However, the conviction that the person is above all a *receiver* can very well remain here to the end.

Translated by John Bowden

Notes

1. Though communities with a loose structure and little sense of ceremonial, like the Pygmies, have no ancestor worship.
2. E. Bolaji Idowu, *African Traditional Religion. A Definition*, London 1973, 187.
3. R. Jaulin, *La mort Sara*, Paris 1971, 378.
4. M. Y. Nabofa, 'Erhi and Eschatology', in *Traditional Religion in West Africa*, ed. E. A. Ade-Adegbola, Accra 1983, 311–12.
5. See e.g. Marc Augé, *Pouvoirs de vie, pouvoirs de mort*, Paris 1977, 96–7.
6. D. Zahan, 'Aspects de la réincarnation et de la vie mystique chez le Bambara', in *Réincarnation et vie mystique en Afrique noire*, Colloque de Strasbourg 1963, Paris 1965, 20. See also id., *Religion, spiritualité et pensée africaines*, Paris 1970.
7. In May 1992 there was a congress at the Free University of Amsterdam on the disturbance of multiple personality. Anyone who suffers from this disturbance harbours several egos, each with its own will, taste, view, time of life. Such a person is the host of several personalities which take control in turn. Therapy tries to bring out the whole 'team' of personalities in the host and make him or her a whole.
8. 'Life, in the strictest sense, is not individual and derived, and death takes place as a secondary manifestation, the individual' (Jaulin, *La mort Sara*, n.3, 402). 'The genius of the family never dies: it keeps manifesting itself in unbroken sequence of offspring' (among the Nupe). Thus E. Bolaji Idowu, *African Traditional Religion* (n.1), 188. Cf. also L.–V. Thomas, 'L'Eschatologie: performance et mutation', in *Reincarnation, Immortalité, Résurrection*, Brussels 1988, 12.
9. Marguérite Dupire, 'Numination, reincarnation et/ou ancêtre tutélaire? Un mode de survie. L'exemple des Serer Ndout (Sénégal)', *L'Homme* 22, 1982, 1, 5. See also Richard Friedli, *Zwischen Himmel und Hölle – Die Reinkarnation. Ein religionswissenschaftliches Handbuch*, Fribourg, CH 1986, 93.
10. L.–V. Thomas and R. Luneau, *La terre africaine et ses religions*, Paris 1975, 98.
11. According to others, for example the Urhobo (Nigeria), ancestors seem to be confronted with the choice of either being reincarnated or remaining in the hereafter (see n.1).
12. J. P. Kiernan, 'The "Problem of Evil" in the Context of Ancestral Intervention in the Affairs of the Living in Africa', *Man*, NS 17, 1982, 292–3, draws a distinction between 'affinal' and 'lineal' ancestors. All the latter are regarded as preservers of the family.
13. According to the Bambara (of Mali), however, any child is the heir of two living principles of someone who has died just before the birth of the child. See Germaine Dieterlen, *Essai sur la religion Bambara*, Brussels 1988, 83.
14. See Dupire, 'Numination' (n.9 above).

15. The newborn child is also thoroughly inspected among the Urhobo of Nigeria. The parents try to discover whether it is a reincarnation of a dead member of the family. Physical characteristics of the baby can indicate this, and also the behaviour displayed by the growing child.

16. According to Bolaji Idowu, *African Traditional Religion* (n.2), successive reincarnation without limit is possible. The ancestors can reincarnate themselves *'ad infinitum'* (188: 'rather exhausting', he adds).

17. As if ancestors and little children are holding each other by the hand (and thus 'encircle the adults', as Jaulin, *La mort Sara*, n.3, 379, puts it). A. Retel-Laurentin and R. Bangbanzi have indicated the link between increasing childlessness and doubt about ancestor worship in the east of the Central African Republic. Cf. 'Les Nzakaras et leurs ancêtres', *Cahiers des Etudes Africaines* 6, 1966, no.3, 463–53. Descendants – a potential work-force – are the most important means of existence for the economy of non-industrialized societies.

Reincarnation in Connection with Spiritism and Umbanda

Rogier van Rossum

The main impression left by the commemoration of the five hundred years of oppression and Christianization of Latin America is the dispute over the restoration of their rights to the original population, and to the African population which still bears the stigmata of centuries of slavery. I hope that this also includes what a recent French volume of essays refers to as 'Our Mestizo America'.[1] The question that will concern us in this article, the distinctively Brazilian development of the nineteenth-century European idea of reincarnation, certainly has a lot to do with mixing and fusion. Millions of Brazilians have a very specific expectation for the future: on the basis of the present-day mixing of races a new humanity will develop in Brazil in the third millennium. Spiritism and Umbanda already have the makings of a universalistic religion here. So God remains Brazilian.[2]

The idea of reincarnation is a basic one in the spiritist movement in Brazil, which emerges more strongly here than elsewhere as a religious movement. Within Umbanda, an expression of the process of religious ferment in Brazil's great cities, the idea of reincarnation remains one of the forces which holds teaching together.

So both spiritism and Umbanda must be presented, if we are to see the idea of reincarnation functioning. Of course this doctrinal presentation does not show the full influence of the two neo-religious movements (in rites, ethics and mysticism). I am using the term 'neo-religious' as I find it in the study by Ingo Wulfhorst, 'The Spiritualist-Christian Orders. Origin and Manifestations of a Neo-Religious Movement in Brazil'.[3] There is as yet no Catholic study to match this Reformation one.

Until very recently the Catholic approach to spiritism and Umbanda was very heavily apologetic. The great master of this apologetics, who indeed was appointed to it by the young Brazilian conference of bishops, was Bonaventura Kloppenburg.[4] From 1970 the Centro Latino-Americano de Parapsicologia functioned in connection with the Catholic University of São Paulo as a parapsychological complement. The material of both was much used in a great many educational campaigns.[5] What one misses here is a real history-of-religions approach, rather than all kinds of fruits of scientific studies from an anthropological, sociological and psychological perspective. Moreover these are linked above all with the African contribution to these neo-religious movements and are treated in an approach which is more related to reality only in the studies of C. P. F. de Camargo,[6] with his standpoint that there is a 'mediumistic continuum' between very different Afro-American cult-places on the one hand and spiritist groups on the other. However, de Camargo develops only some of the therapeutic influence of this continuum and its function in providing social compensation, not the religious function. The Brazilian Ortiz[7] works further on this continuum in a first attempt to describe Umbanda 'from the inside out' in a field between two poles, one more Western and one less Western. Umbanda, he argues, has never been the expression of the lowest strata of the Brazilian proletariat but is the result of a dialectical movement of the 'becoming white' and 'becoming black' of Brazilian society. Thus he sees the explanation for the origin and development of Umbanda as the new religion of a new Brazilian society in a far-ranging syncretism of the white and black population. Ortiz demonstrates that from the beginning Umbanda was bound up with urbanization and industrialization. Thus at least the Brazilian city must not be interpreted as the centre of secularization, as often happens.[8]

Sparta's book *A Dança dos Orixas*[9] seems to be a turning point in the Catholic approach, although this more positive direction seems to apply more to the Afro-Brazilian part than to the spiritist part. A great silence seems to fall over that.

I. 'God, Christ, love': spiritism and reincarnation in Brazil

In its present-day form, too, Brazilian spiritism, which is much more developed in religious terms than European or North American spiritism, feels itself to be a scientific system in search of unassailable scientific proofs for the authenticity of the revelation of spirits and their messages. Here this so-called scientific spiritism still constantly uses as a starting point what it calls 'the animistic interpretation'; in other words, the phenomena are based on the extraordinary capacity of the human soul (*anima*, hence animistic). Great caution and restraint are required in the interpretation of the empirical material. [9] Above all it has been necessary to keep strictly to the 'animistic' hypotheses; in other words, only the phenomena which are regarded as 'authentic' are derived from 'spirits' and therefore regarded as 'spiritist' or as 'spiritualistic interpretation'.

The homeland of all these concepts is nineteenth-century Europe. In Brazil the French pedagogue Léon Hippolyte Dénizard Rivail (1804–1869) is regarded as *the* representation of this spiritualistic interpretation. He is known everywhere under his pseudonym Alain Kardec. Already as a Catholic youth at a Protestant Swiss school he found the Christian confessions intolerable and therefore cherished his ideal of 'reforming religion'. In 1853 he came under the influence of 'Messmerism', a movement of healing derived from the theory of 'animal magnetism': there is only one sickness and one cure, sickness as a destruction of the harmony with nature, and healing as a restoration of the relationship which has been damaged. Messmer's pupils Puységur and Deleuse investigated the parapsychological phenomena which appear with soothsaying and the conjuring up of spirits and the writings of a philosophical and religious nature associated with this, which derive from spirits. Here the idea of reincarnation began to play a decisive role and made Messmerism take a new course. Rivail then gradually began to devote himself to an empirical investigation of spiritist phenomena. He wrote his first study of them, *Le livre des esprits*, in 1857. The book is meant to be a systematic codification of 'the doctrine of spirits': i.e., the spirits give answers to more than a dozen questions put to them by mediums in the form of a catechism. Above all these are questions about the immortality of the soul, the nature of spirits, their relationship with human beings, the moral law, earthly and future life, the future of humankind.

The day of the publication of this book, 18 April 1857, is regarded by Brazilian spiritists as the day of the foundation of 'the modern spiritualistic movement'. Kardec's subsequent study, *Le livre des mediums*, gives instructions to mediums and those who conjure up spirits as to how experimental spiritism works. Finally, Kardec wrote *L'Evangile selon le Spiritisme*. This is a spiritist interpretation of the four Gospels: spiritism as 'the third revelation' after those of Moses and Jesus Christ.

The three books together form the canon of Brazilian spiritism. In the middle of the nineteenth century there was close contact between Brazilian society and modern French developments. The ideas of Auguste Comte were taken up in the largely anti-clerical upper classes. The same thing happened with the works of Kardec. Propaganda for them received a good deal of support when the works were burned in 1861 in the latest Spanish *auto da fé*. Later Kardecism became above all a middle-class phenomenon. The Federaçao Espírita Brasiliera (FEB) arose as early as 1884. In 1980 this linked more than 5000 Kardecist groups spread throughout the country. From 1940 on, in censuses people could call themselves spiritists as well as Catholics or Protestants.

With a number of observers[10] I see the prime attraction of Kardecism as being its teaching about love of neighbour, which is practised every day. Nor does this stop at teaching. Brazil is full of spiritist institutions: homes for the elderly and for children, first-aid posts and hospitals, places of instruction and work-places. And any Kardecist asked about the motives behind this unsubsidized and extensive charitable work will point to the Sermon on the Mount and of course speak of 'Christian spiritism'.

Furthermore one can easily go into the spiritist centres and find that word and prayer are not restricted to particular individuals. Anyone can pray and interpret scripture.

Through national and regional congresses, special weeks and so-called 'evangelization campaigns', the FEB sees to the dissemination and proper interpretation of the Kardecist message. The FEB has more than 100 programmes on radio and television.

Brazilian Kardecism also strictly observes the two kinds of weekly meeting which Kardec had envisaged, namely sessions 'for practising neighbourly love' and sessions 'to develop the capacity of being a medium'. Of course the former sessions have a much stronger religious colour and atmosphere. With their strongly mystical and therapeutic function they have a fixed ritual, with 'spiritual redemption' as their centre and aim. The 'development sessions', which are also held weekly, are, as has been said, aimed at the development of critical reflection by the medium on spirit messages. Here the reading of the New Testament plays an important role in lectures and group discussions. Moreover the aim is the development of spiritism as 'Christian spiritism'.

Kardecism did in Brazil what the Theosophical and Anthroposophical movement did in nineteenth-century Europe, i.e. introduced and developed its own idea of reincarnation. I can best indicate the distinctive Brazilian views by first presenting the summary that Kranenborg[11] gives of the European Theosophical development. The world is an emanation from God, matter and the body are from a lower level. God and human beings are identical in nature. Human beings have more than one life, but in contrast to Hinduism there is always growth, progress and evolution in successive lives. Thus no rebirth takes place in an animal. The nucleus of human beings is unique and is not given over to corruption. The law of cause and effect, the law of karma, is vital. Jesus is the one who gives hope, courage, insight and help in personal development. Jesus is the incarnation of the universal cosmic Christ-principle. Vicarious suffering, forgiveness and union are explicitly denied. Human beings must work out their own redemption. They choose their own way. Karma is repentance, restoration. One must do one's duty and therefore love one's neighbours. One can help one's fellow human beings to work out their karma and that also helps one to work out one's own karma. Human beings are in a network of cosmic relationships, and occupy the highest place in the process of evolution. If we set Kardecism against this background, the unity with its time of origin (middle of the nineteenth century) is evident, but so too is a great difference; Kardecism begins with 'spirits', not with human beings.

Within Kardecism the material, visible world is contrasted with this immaterial, invisible, spiritual and original world. The spirits take on 'a material covering' on earth only for a particular time and then once again resume their original freedom. All spirits were originally created equal by God, and all are also involved in spiritual evolution towards ultimate perfection. But from that original development they develop at different rates towards the final goal 'in the practice of love of neighbour'. This development ('evolution') stands under the *lex divina* ('the spiritual law'), 'the law of cause and effect', understood as the inexorable law of the retribution of good and evil deeds. The principle of reincarnation on earth aids the process of the purification of spirits on the ladder of progress towards ultimate perfection, which one day will be achieved by all spirits. The earth is seen as a planet of expiation and learning on the spirits' way towards purification and consummation.

As material beings, men and women who live on earth, the planet of expiation, have their physical bodies; their souls, as the immaterial being in which the immortal spirit dwells as a divine spark; and their perispiritus. This is a half spiritual and half material covering which holds together soul and body and which detaches itself from the physical body at death as being the coarsest covering. For the disincarnate spirit the perispiritus forms an ethereal body which is normally invisible, but can become visible, audible and tangible in communication by and with spirits. In disincarnation the soul which has done well in its trials returns to the spiritual fatherland from which it came. After a shorter or longer time it incarnates itself again in order to achieve a higher state of consciousness. However, after its disincarnation a soul which has not done well in its earthly time of trial finds itself in the utmost confusion and does not succeed in detaching itself from its earthly bonds. As a wandering spirit it ultimately gets in the grips of evil and thus as a 'suffering spirit' can do evil to human beings. Only a new reincarnation offers such a spirit the possibility of developing further.

The sphere of the world consists of various heavenly bodies which are inhabited by the disincarnate spirits, each in accordance with its own phase of development. The incorporeal 'false spirits' are not bound to such a fixed space and appear everywhere as an 'invisible population'. Wandering round in darkness over the earth, they sometimes appear to human beings to influence them for good or evil. In conformity with the different phases in the process of evolution there is thus a multiplicity of inhabited worlds in the process of evolution; the higher have an increasingly attractive 'landscape'. Ultimately the soul which has evolved into pure spirit returns to God's presence and is withdrawn from the law of cause and effect and thus freed from the cycle of reincarnation. However, it can reincarnate later for the benefit of the evolution of humankind and the earth and undertake a 'divine mission'. These 'pure spirits' support the incarnate and disincarnate spirits as 'angel guardians and forerunners'. Their communication serves towards mutual revaluation. Its content relates to the praxis of love of neighbour within their spiritual evolution, with the ultimate aim of detachment from the cycle of reincarnation.

Third revelation

As I have already indicated, Kardecism regards itself as the third revelation after the revelation to Moses and to Jesus, which as such is directed towards the 'rediscovery and renewal' of the divine law. This law consists of love of God as the supreme being, and doing good as the normal basic condition for achieving happiness in a future life. Kardecism sums up the whole of this law, which is also called 'natural law', with an explicit reference to the 'morals of Jesus', in the command to love one's neighbour. 'The practice of love of neighbour is the practice of the one true religion.' As a result of this, people can check the unregulated drives in their lives and pass through the stages of their spiritual, evolutionary course. With a nod to the Catholic church, it is said that 'there is no salvation without love of neighbour'.

Now this 'natural law' was not just revealed to Moses and Jesus. It has come to human beings in all times and cultures through messages from the invisible world. Therefore spiritism can be found in all faiths of all times. 'Third revelation' means that Cardecism offers a scientific summary of all these revelations. It is therefore best for spiritists to be members of a church, as long the church does not exclude them.

While the first and second revelations took place through the incarnation of one prophetic spirit (Moses, Jesus), this third revelation came about through an accumulation of messages from the spirits to the mediums. However, as the 'doctrine of the spirits', the 'doctrine of spiritism', it is confessed by Jesus in his farewell discourse (John 16.12ff.) as perfect knowledge of the truth revealed to Kardec by the Spirit of truth. Spiritism follows in the footsteps of scripture.

Kardec predicted that in a few generations spiritism would spread as the 'spiritual renewal of the divine law'. As 'the religious reformation', 'universal belief', 'the bond which unites humankind', it would be the one true religion based on the original and unfalsified gospel.

Or, in other Kardecistic terms, it is the 'revelation authenticated by Christ', a religious doctrine 'without dogmas, without liturgy, without symbols, without an organized priesthood'.

But on other occasions Kardecism sometimes presents itself as 'simply morality'. As the third revelation, Kardecism seems itself called to the spiritual renewal of the divine natural law and thus regards itself as 'the restoration of the religion of Jesus'. According to this natural law the practice of the love of neighbour, already lived out in an exemplary way by Jesus, is the one way of salvation for incarnate and disincarnate spirits.

Finally, Jesus is seen as one of the many divine 'prophets' and 'masters' sent to earth. Death and resurrection drop right out of his life story, since they do not fit into the notion of evolution resting on karma. Grace, reconciliation, cross, fit into it even less. Individuals save themselves. From scripture it is the Decalogue and the morality of Jesus which make an impact.

II. The transition from reincarnation to Umbanda

Since the studies by C. P. de Camargo,[12] his standpoint relating to the existence of a 'mediumistic continuum' which runs from Kardecism on the one hand to Umbanda on the other has been increasingly confirmed. Of course, Cardecism, as indicated above, forms a clearly defined pole, whereas Umbanda is still in the full flood of development. Nevertheless it can be demonstrated that the increasing doctrinal consistency of Umbanda is provided not by popular Catholic or Afro-Brazilian key religious data, but by the world of reincarnation.

Our brief account of this way of understanding continues as it were to hang in the air since there is no room here to go into Afro-Brazilian syncretism, which arose out of the two-fold religious allegiance that Brazil has had from the time of the introduction of African slaves.[13] Since we are concerned with the idea of reincarnation, which is alien to the African religious tradition, we shall have to keep to some basic doctrinal principles, which are generally described as 'Lei de Umbanda' (the law of Umbanda); this is summed up, in a way which is clearly influenced by Kardecism, as 'practice of love of neighbour'. What is meant here is that the only way of redemption (= development) to God is by means of the practice of love of neighbour. Divine beings and spirits offer guidance and help in this.

Wulfhorst[14] cites the following Umbandist creed: 'I believe in God, the omnipotent and highest, in the Orixas and in the divine spirits which according to God's will brought us to life; I believe in the rebirth of the soul and the divine righteousness in conformity with the law of return; I believe in communication with the leaders who went before us on the way of love of neighbour by practising the good; I believe in invocation and the prayer of intercession, and in sacrifices as well as in the practices of faith; I believe in Umbanda as a religion of redemption which can bring us on the way of development to Orixa Father.'

It emerges from this creed and from a number of passages like the Catecismo de Umbanda that the Umbanda theologians go much further than the assimilation of Catholic customs and saints' names, the practice by which the period of slavery saved Afro-Brazilian religion. Their approach to the Orixas is far removed from their African origin and content, and also from the way in which they function in the Candomblé. Here the Orixas are the highest beings, and any person, not just the initiates, has an Orixa as a personal 'guide'. If such an Orixa incorporates himself in the cult in a person, it can make this person an instrument with no will of his or her own. The supreme Orixa (Oxalá or Orixalá) is connected with Jesus. When the Umbanda decided to hold its first national congress in Rio de Janeiro in 1948, Jesus was referred to as 'the supreme leader of Umbanda-spiritism in whose service the spirits are in a very high state of evolution like Caboclos and Pretos Velhos'.

The Orixas are incorporated with the incarnate and discarnate spirits into the Kardecist evolutionary hierarchy of the spirits. One can see in any Umbanda cult how such a paramilitary hierarchical order works. The main idea behind it, 'spiritual relations between God and humankind', is developed further with purely Kardecist elements of rebirth, karma law and the practice of love of neighbour. These form the basic ingredients of the evolutionary redemptive doctrine of Umbanda, seen as a divine law which nothing can escape.

Thus the fourth resolution of the Umbanda congress mentioned above states: 'the doctrine of Umbanda is built on the principle of the reincarnation of the spirit in successive incarnations as necessary steps in its evolution.' Reincarnation serves as expiation for the faults and errors of previous incarnations; it gives people the possibility of progressing and developing through suffering and through the practice of love of neighbour; it also helps spirits who have already achieved a higher level to perform important 'missions'. What is decisive is that the incarnate spirit is recognized and practises the law of the love of neighbour in which the whole of Umbanda can be summarized.[15]

> 'Its philosophy consists of recognizing again human nature as a divine particle which streams in clarity and purity from the divine, and at the end of the necessary cycle is taken up again in the same state of holiness and purity, achieved by its own effort and will.'[16]

Such considerations are aimed at giving Umbanda a place in the general religious history of humankind (the images of an Umbanda cult-place conjure that up), and begin to derive the origin and content of the African word Umbanda from the Sanskrit, rendering it as 'divine principle, emanating light, ever-flowing source of life, ongoing evolution'.

III. Neo-religious movements

The self-understanding of Brazilian Kardecism and Umbanda may not be limited to their mediumistic therapeutic function.[17] Wulfhorst says quite rightly that in both cases we have syncretistic neo-religious movements. Salvation is seen as the mediumistic evolutionary way of redemption of the immortal spirit (soul) to God. Healing is just part of this way. Both movements present themselves as the universal religion of future humanity. In Kardecism that perspective is built on a spiritism which is already practised universally, but awaits its scientific clarification; in Umbanda the notion of the future is based on its composition, on its syncretistic union with all religions and philosophies. I have already indicated that such perspectives 'work' and gain a following in a multiracial country like Brazil.

To return to the term 'neo-religious movements', which was used by Ernst Dammann in his *Grundriss der Religionsgeschichte*[18] and is also used by Wulfhorst[19] for the Umbanda. In my view the religious approach to Kardecism and Umbanda is the only correct one if one wants to make real contact from the church with these movements which count a significant part of the church among their clientele. The term 'new religious movement' starts from the fact that here we do not have a religion which is fundamentally new and emerging for the first time. It relates to religious movements which form in the sphere of the so-called classical world religions. They differ by being a reinterpretation, innovation, completion and updating of existing classical religion. They usually take shape as a situational innovatory movement on the basis of encounter and confrontation with other cultures and religions, often at a time of rapid social change. The interaction, reciprocal penetration and integration which comes about as a result leads to syncretism. In any case, a new religion is experienced by its members as something new in comparison to what they are familiar with. Sooner or later the neo-religious movement develops into an independent organization and often claims to be the true, up-to-date form of the old religion and also the modern universal religion for all humankind.

As long as Brazil continued to live in the old social patterns, i.e. up to the industrialization and above all urbanization which began to transform the country and its inhabitants from the 1940s onwards, it had a popular Catholic culture, which either assimilated Afro-Brazilian elements or tolerated them in a disinterested way. Hardly any account was taken of the vitality of the Afro-Brazilian cults supported by free negroes or the power of attraction for Catholics of particular therapeutic skills closely connected with African religiosity. The so-called 'passes' which are now one of the attractions of Kardecist healing sessions were not unknown to the African cults. The Romanization of the Brazilian church from the end of the nineteenth century did not increase the capacity of the church to perceive these questions of salvation and damnation which were often alive within the church. When in August 1953 the Brazilian bishops began to organize a 'national campaign against spiritist heresy' from the National Secretariat for the Defence of Faith and Morals, the lack of religious training among Catholics was a central issue. With impressive documentation Kloppenburg succeeds in bringing together spiritism, Umbanda and reincarnation and testing the documentation by the Bible, the church fathers and dogmatics. However, he does not seem anywhere to have any sense of the plausibility of the idea of reincarnation, of the reflections of people who see their society undergoing deep change and do not want to drop the religious element. Has the church an explanation, like reincarnation, of why things happen as they do? Does it go into the human need to sort out all the connections by assuming that there will be satisfaction in a subsequent life for sins committed and recognized? Does it answer the question why many lives end incomplete, many tasks are unfulfilled? Can there be eternal damnation after one life? Is not reincarnation full of compassion, in that people can make good their mistakes?

Neither of the two neo-religious movements says that you have to leave the church for an answer to such questions, but they do claim to have an answer themselves.

Translated by John Bowden

Notes

1. A. Renimche, *Notre Amérique métisse. Cinq cents ans après les Latino-Américains parlent aux Européens*, Paris 1992.
2. I. Wulfhorst, *Der spiritualistisch-christlichen Orden. Ursprung und Erscheinungs-formen einer neureligiösen Bewegung in Brasilien*, Erlangen 1985, 71.
3. Ibid., 1.
4. B. Kloppenburg's works appeared in the 1950s in the journal *Revista Eclesiastica Brasileira* published by Vozes and later in their series Vozes em Defesa da Fé.
5. Wulfhorst, *Spiritualistisch-christliche Orden* (n.2), 255–9.
6. C. P. F. de Camargo, *Kardecismo e Umbanda, Uma interpretação sociologica*, São Paulo 1961.
7. R. Ortiz, *A morte branca do feiticeiro negro. Umbanda, integração de uma religião numa sociedade de classes*, Petropolis 1978.
8. Ibid., 89.
9. F. Sparta, *A dança dos Orixas, As relíquias brasileiras da Afro-Asia pré-bíblica*, São Paulo 1970.
10. Wulfhorst, *Spiritualistisch-christliche Orden* (n.2), 29.
11. R. Kranenborg, 'Christianity and Reincarnation', in J. Gort et al. (eds.), *Dialogue and Syncretism. An Interdisciplinary Approach*, Amsterdam 1989, 181–2.
12. C. P. F. de Camargo and J. Labben, 'Aspects socio-culturelles du Spiritisme au Brésil', *Social Compass* 7, 1960, 407–30.
13. R. Bastide, *Les Religions africaines au Brésil*, Paris 1960, 151–74.
14. Wulfhorst, *Spiritualistisch-christliche Orden* (n.2), 66.
15. There is a review of this congress by Kloppenburg in *REB* 12, 1952, 93.
16. U. Fischer, *Zur Liturgie des Umbandakultes. Eine Untersuchung zu den Kultriten oder Amtshandlungen der synkretistischen Neureligion de Umbanda in Brasilien*, Leiden 1970, 110.
17. Wulfhorst, *Spiritualistisch-christlichen Orden* (n.2), 71.
18. E. Dammann, *Grundriss der Religiongeschichte*, Stuttgart 1972, 101.
19. Wulfhorst, *Spiritualistisch-christliche Orden* (n.2), 71.

II · Theological Orientations on Resurrection

Reincarnation or Resurrection?
Resurrection and Biblical Apocalyptic

Karl Löning

From the beginning, the Christian world-view was set in the context of an expectation of the end of the world, history and human life. Hope for the resurrection of the dead came into being in this context and cannot be detached from it. This article will sketch out in six theses the main aspects of the Jewish-Christian belief in resurrection which need particularly to be taken into account in a discussion about reincarnation or resurrection, against the background of texts from early Judaism and the earliest Christianity.

> *Thesis 1: Belief in the resurrection developed relatively late in the history of the biblical tradition. However, it is not an alien body there, but the expression of original elements of belief in Yahweh.*

The earliest clear evidence for belief in the resurrection of the dead is Dan.12.2f. ('those who sleep in the dust of the earth'). The final redaction of the book of Daniel took place between 168 and 164 BCE. This statement comes from one of the latest parts of the book. As the preceding context indicates, the historical background to Dan.12.1f. is the religious and political persecutions under the Seleucid Diadoche king Antiochus IV Epiphanes and the beginning of the Maccabaean revolt. Here the expectation of resurrection is quite concretely embedded in an attempt to come to terms with contemporary history and is itself an aspect of the rescue of the Jewish people from the current threat to its historical existence as the people of God (cf.12.1). Here we have an expression of a classic central aspect of belief in Yahweh, which is based on the Exodus experience and the way in which it was repeated in the history of Israel. At this point the motive of the raising of the dead in itself is possibly of Iranian origin, having found its way into early Jewish thought by means of Hellenism. However, as we can see here, it is no indication of a readiness for religious assimilation; on the contrary, it is an element of the conflict with Hellenism represented by the Seleucid Antiochus. The same is also true in principle of early traces of belief in the resurrection in the Old Testament: Hosea 6.1–3, the only pre-exilic text of this kind, and the Isaiah Apocalypse (Isa.26, around 300 BCE) are influenced by the Canaanite vegetation myth; and the vision of the revival of the dead bones in Ezekiel 37 is probably influenced by the Osiris myth. However, the scope of the statements is not a result of 'alien influence'. In Ezek.37 the expectation does not relate to the awakening of the dead in the eternal kingdom of Osiris in the other world, but to the new historical future of the Jewish people brought about by God after the exile. God's influence extends beyond the boundary of death. This is made manifest in the history of the people. To this degree, belief in the resurrection in the Jewish-Christian tradition is biblical from the start.

> *Thesis 2: The content of the early Jewish and earliest Christian belief in the resurrection of the dead does not imply a dichotomistic anthropology with the notion of an immortal human soul, but relates totally to the physical human being.*

Belief in the resurrection of the dead is not a consequence of anthropological views, e.g. that as spiritual beings men and women are not identical with their material existence, that they are immortal in their authentic being, that as the real nucleus of the person the soul is only provisionally connected with the material body, that the body as a prison prevents the soul from achieving its authentic mode of being, or the like. Rather, the doctrine of the immortality of the soul is conversely a secondary, post-biblical theory as compared with the doctrine of the resurrection, one which strives to achieve a balance between Jewish-Christian belief in resurrection and Hellenistic anthropology.

According to early Jewish anthropology the resurrection of the dead does not lie in the sphere of human nature or potential human development, and to this degree is neither a natural nor a supernatural procedure, but an action of God in human beings. Given human nature, the resurrection of the flesh is in fact an impossibility. For a body to rise from the tomb and to continue to live as a human being is an impossibility not only for our thought with its scientific orientation but also for early Jewish anthropology. But the provocative oddness of this notion is used specifically to indicate the power that God has over death. God can raise up children to Abraham from stones (cf. Matt.3.9; Luke 3.8). Human beings are taken from the earth and return to it; their life is breathed into them as a fleeting breath. It is inherent in the nature of human beings to give back the life that they have received in death as a gift of the Creator over which they have no control; it is inherent in the freedom of the creative action of God to call life into being and to take it back without leaving a trace. By nature nothing is left of human beings. The belief that the world of the dead must eventually give up the dead (cf. I Enoch 51.1; IV Ezra 7.32; SyrBar 21.23f.; Rev.20.12–15) is an expression of the hope that God will bring this about. Even more it is in God's power alone to remedy the injustice done to the righteous and to restore their tortured bodies to them (cf. II Macc.7.22f.; 14.37–46). Speculations of later texts about an intermediate state in which the souls of the dead await the day of their resurrection in (various) heavenly chambers and similar borrowings from Hellenistic anthropology (cf. I Enoch 22.1–14; 39.3–13; IV Ezra 7.88,90f.; SyrBar 30.24) serve to reconcile the original approach of the notion of resurrection with the experience of ongoing time. Despite tendencies hostile to the body in some of these texts, the preservation of separated souls in their chambers does not represent an ascent to a higher form of being. Moreover evil souls are separated from righteous souls.

Thesis 3: In early Jewish and earliest Christian tradition the resurrection of the dead is connected with the expectation of the eschatological end of history specifically in respect of the present, which is experienced as being chaotic. Over against this, it asserts the meaning of historical human existence, particularly in face of the suffering of the righteous.

The resurrection of the flesh is no more inherent in the nature of creaturely human beings as a possibility for their own development than the rule of God is inherent in human history. According to the world-view of apocalyptic, the rule of God and life in the age of the kingdom of God are not the result to which human history is moving individually and collectively. The continuum of one state giving way to another in the world is exclusively throught of in terms of God, who appoints and deposes kings in accordance with his own hidden plan, without the intervention of human hands, until the final establishment of the kingdom of God (cf.Dan.2.21,45). Human history and human historical existence take place under conditions which are hostile to God, imposed by each particular world power in the time appointed for it. That the empires giving way to one another develop their power historically is God's plan;

how they do it is increasingly contrary to God. In the end God's rule is a rescue from the failure of history.

A perception of historical conditions and processes which takes this approach does not find any prelude to the rule of God in history but expects this as salvation specifically at the catastrophic end of all the ages of the world. Contemporary history is followed with intensified attention; not, however, in the certainty of seeing God's hand in it, but conversely in the anxious hope that the unspeakable suffering of the elect will not at last provoke God's mercy. That one can hope for this is not the result of any estimation of the balance of power within history and of any shifting of this, possibly by one's own resistance. Rather, the possibility and the power to suffer and resist, in faithfulness to God, are grounded in trust in the faithfulness of God to those who fear him. Knowledge that although God never puts an end to the violence of the wicked, God's justice determines all things, is the starting point for the view that the chaos of history with its catastrophes has a time appointed and planned by God, and that the suffering of the pious can therefore be endured because it is transitory. Belief in the resurrection *of the righteous* is an expression of this trust. Here resurrection is of interest less as an external event of revival than primarily as the definitive rehabilitation of belief in Yahweh as the superior form of insight and justice (cf. Dan.12.3) in the final fate of his martyred witnesses.

> *Thesis 4: The earliest Christian belief in the resurrection of Jesus presupposes the early Jewish belief in the general resurrection of the dead and brings it up to date in a way which is constitutive of the earliest Christian understanding of God.*

The preaching of Jesus speaks in many ways of the coming of the kingdom of God and the nearness of God to his creation. However, the resurrection of the dead does not seem to have been a central theme in it. The death and resurrection of Jesus stand at the centre of the earliest Christian proclamation. This is possible and understandable because in the meantime the public activity of Jesus and his death and resurrection had provided a context which could be summed up in belief in the resurrection of Jesus: the earliest form in which the primitive Christian Easter faith found expression is the so-called *pistis* formula, a stereotyped phrase which formulates the Easter event theocentrically as a statement about God who 'has raised him (Jesus) from the dead' (I Thess.1.9f.; Rom.10.9; II Cor.4.14; Gal.1.1; Rom.4.24; 8.11; Col.2.12; Eph.1.19f.; I Peter 1.21). It is earlier than the composite confessional formula in I Cor.15.3–5, and its nucleus can be derived from the contemporary Jewish language of prayer. The second of the Eighteen Benedictions reads: 'You are a mighty hero . . . , you feed the living and bring the dead to life . . . Praise be to you, Yahweh, you bring the dead to life.' The earliest Christian confession of God who has raised Jesus from the dead presupposes the understanding of God in this prayer with its apocalyptic mould. Here we can recognise the connection to which the statement about the resurrection owes its central position in earliest Christian faith, namely the connection between the action of God in Jesus and the apocalyptic hope for the salvation of all the righteous or believers (cf. Rom.4.17–25; 8.9–11). This context makes the action of God in the crucified Jesus the revelation of his definitive will for salvation.

Thesis 5: The Easter stories of the New Testament Gospels reflect the significance of the resurrection of Jesus from the aspect of participation through knowledge of revelation.

Radical rationalistic biblical criticism was right in its thesis that as historical evidence the New Testament Easter stories do not provide any proof of the resurrection of Jesus. However, the presupposition that they are to be read as historical accounts rests on a false estimation of the texts. These already reflect its significance on the basis of Easter faith.

Mark 16.1–8 describes the discovery of the empty tomb as a failed quest for Jesus in the wrong place. The appearance of the angel clad in white at the place of death and his invitation to follow Jesus to Galilee become an impulse to the reader – not least because of the flight of the women – to take up the quest for Jesus, in the sense of the discipleship of the cross, in the right direction.

Luke 24 picks up this theme and enlarges on it in a story which develops the dimensions of the Easter faith in three phases: 1. the death of Jesus is the predestined suffering of the Son of Man at human hands. This understanding rests on the recollection of Jesus' words of revelation (cf. 24.7f.) about himself and the repudiation of his mission. 2. The resurrection of Jesus is the fulfilment of the hope of his disciples for the redemption of Israel which was apparently frustrated in his death. The prototypical raising of Jesus is to this degree the fulfilment of the 'scriptures' which contain God's promise (cf. 24.25–27). 3. These two aspects of Easter faith are finally (24.44–49) identified as one and the same knowledge of revelation and handed on to the disciples as witnesses, to proclaim to the ends of the earth. Here the mission of Jesus as God's last messenger reached its goal.

Matthew 28 certainly does not take up the theme of the quest for the risen Jesus. Here the Risen One appears immediately after the angelophany to the women coming from the tomb and is recognized by the two women Easter witnesses without any help. Matthew is also an exception in that he depicts the resurrection primarily as an external event, as the earthquake-like shattering of the previous power-relationships documented by the seal on the tomb indicates. But even this exception proves the rule, that all the canonical Gospels understand the resurrection of Jesus primarily as the revelation of God. The new era which begins with the death and resurrection of Jesus is not considered in accordance with the traditional apocalyptic scheme as the end of Roman rule, but as the future in which the peoples will become disciples by being given the teaching of Jesus.

The aspect of participation based on knowledge of revelation becomes particularly clear in the Johannine account of the passion and resurrection of Jesus. In the Johannine perspective the death of Jesus is the going to the Father, the way which is opened up by the departure of the Son and is made manifest to believers in the word of Jesus. The new immediate relationship to God which the Exalted One communicates in the Spirit is the abiding of the disciples in the Word of Jesus.

So the resurrection of Jesus is narrated by all the canonical Gospels as the event in which the power and will of God to consummate history is revealed through the liberation of human beings from death to life. Here the corresponding awareness of hope in Israel on the basis of its historical experiences with God (promise) is eschatologically and definitively confirmed and appropriated as knowledge (fulfilment). Precisely for that reason the resurrection as such is nowhere narrated as a historical event in the Gospels, the traces of which can later be viewed in a museum of biblical antiquity, thanks to their confirmation by evangelists and exegetes.

Thesis 6: The anthropologically holistic approach of early Jewish belief to the resurrection of the flesh is not given up in the context of the New Testament soteriologies.

With the earliest Christian belief in the resurrection of Jesus is combined the imminent expectation of his return as the Son of Man-judge who finally ushers in the kingdom of God. The earliest Christian hope also knows of this link in connection with the believers' expectation of salvation. From the start the earliest Christian belief in Christ is hope both for the imminent parousia of the Kyrios and at the same time for the consummation of the quality of life newly achieved in Christ by participation in his resurrection – now already communicated in baptism. Accordingly, baptism is both a rite of preservation in respect of the eschatological judgment (cf. Acts 2.38) and a mysterious participation in the personal existence of the Risen One which brings about communion (cf. Gal.3.26–28; Rom.6.3f.).

To this degree, the earliest Christian hope of resurrection differs from the traditional apocalyptic view and also from the early Jewish hope of resurrection which developed further at the same time. The case of Jesus is not an isolated precedent for divine rescue from the dead; the example is eschatologically definitive because it is based on specific witness to the imminence of the kingdom of God, on the only Son himself, the last messenger of God's wisdom, in whose mission the reconciled relationship of God to the world as creation has been made manifest. What the earthly Jesus embodies, the Risen One communicates even more through his Spirit. The christological personalization is the element which gives the earliest Christian belief in resurrection the strongest profile over against the apocalyptic tradition and developments in classical Judaism.

The notion of the individual fate of the dead at first retreats in the face of the euphoria of the imminent expectation of the parousia. But grappling with the experience of death within the earliest Christian communities then finds a specific possibility, again in a christological perspective, of expressing a hope which reaches beyond death: when Paul speaks of those members of the community of Thessalonike who have died (or have been killed) as the 'dead in Christ' (I Thess.4.16), he is not speaking of an abode in the world beyond, which could be seen in visionary journeys to heaven; rather, 'in Christ' denotes the novelty of the existence of believers which, in confrontation with the still fatal power of death, is experienced as the communion of living and dead through death which has been overcome in Jesus.

This christologizing does not water down the anthropologically holistic view of resurrection as resurrection of the flesh. Paul defends the holistic approach of resurrection faith to the community of Corinth in the face of Hellenizing reservations on the part of the Corinthians about an idea of consummation which includes the body, when he contrasts the 'corruptibility' of the old being with the 'incorruptibility' of the resurrection body (cf. I Cor.15.24,50–55). The Gospel of John, which is most consistent in transforming belief in the resurrection into the categories of an apocalyptic, wisdom-type conception of revelation, and therefore is occasionally understood as being gnosticizing or anti-gnostic, makes clear in a very drastic way, in its account of the raising of Lazarus, that the confession that believers are now already risen and cannot ever die (cf. John 11.25f.) cannot be detached from the concrete hope that the resurrection of the dead will free the whole person as creature from the stinking gravecloths of death (cf. John 11.38–44). This last of the 'signs' of Jesus leads directly to his passion and glorification.

In general it can be said of the New Testament evidence that despite the beginnings of a detachment on the Christian side of the imminent expectation from its contemporary context in Jewish history, the hope for the resurrection of the dead in the New Testament is still bound up with an apocalyptic perspective on the future. The expected future is not thought of as detached from the corporeal personal and social existence of believers in the present, but is still seen as its consistent consummation by God.

Translated by John Bowden

Bibliography

P. Hoffman (ed.), *Zur neutestamentlichen Überlieferung von der Auferstehung Jesu*, WdF 522, Darmstadt 1988 (with a chronological bibliography, 453–83)

J. Becker, *Auferstehung der Toten im Urchristentum*, SBS 82, Stuttgart 1976

J. Gnilka, 'Contemporary Exegetical Understanding of "the Resurrection of the Body"', *Concilium* 6/10, 1970, 129–41

P. Hoffmann, *Die Toten in Christus. Eine religionsgeschichtliche und exegetische Untersuchung zur paulinischen Eschatologie*, NTA NF 2, Münster [3]1978

J. Kremer, *Die Osterevangelien – Geschichten um Geschichte*, Stuttgart [2]1981

R. Mayer, 'Der Auferstehungsglaube in der iranischen Religion', *Kairos* 7, 1965, 194–207

L. Oberlinner (ed,.), *Auferstehung Jesu – Auferstehung der Christen. Deutungen des Osterglaubens*, QD 105, Freiburg, Basel and Vienna 1986

K. Schubert, 'Die Entwicklung der Auferstehungslehre von der nachexilischen bis zu frührabbinischen Zeit', *BZ* 6, 1962, 177–214

G. Stemberger, 'Das Problem der Auferstehung im AT', *Kairos* 14, 1972, 273–90

– *Der Leib der Auferstehung. Studien zur Anthropologie und Eschatologie des palästinischen Judentums im neutestamentlichen Zeitalter (ca 170 v.Chr – 100 n.Chr)*, AnBib 56, Rome 1972

U. Wilckens, *Auferstehung*, Gütersloh [2]1977

The Early Christian Debate on the Migration of Souls

Norbert Brox

I. The migration of souls is not a Christian theme

Early Christian interest in this theme was not intense. For the early Christians, reincarnation was an exotic and thus an alien idea. Origen already pointed out that it did not appear in the Bible and the Christian tradition; neither of these knew the notion. Where it was mentioned among Christians, which seems to have been seldom enough, there was certainly an awareness that Greek philosophy was concerned with it.[1] So reincarnation was known as an idea among non-Christians. Primarily educated Christians will have come into contact with it. Where their knowledge of philosophy was broad enough, India or Indian philosophy was part of their geographical world-view and their cultural geography as well as Greek cultural history.[2] At any rate this is true of the Alexandrian theologian Origen (died c.154). In his writings he has left behind traces of an interest in Indian ideas and notions, and indeed especially in the doctrine of the migration of souls.[3] This interest was certainly fortified by the fact that he felt provoked by a Christian group which regarded this doctrine as biblical (see below) and wanted to establish it in the church. So the idea of the migration of souls could become very topical.

Origen, who truly had no anxiety about contacts with the non-Christian intellectual world, investigated how compatible a repeated incorporation of human souls was with Christian faith. As a result he is still associated with this theme; however, it is said, wrongly, that he himself advocated this doctrine in Christianity. Origen is then named as a witness to reincarnation in a church which in its early period as a whole advocated and disseminated the idea of the migration of souls, but then later rejected and suppressed it. This is not correct, as will become clear immediately. The remnants of the early Christian debate on the migration of souls are minimal. Apart from Origen and the group already mentioned briefly, only a few names can be given, since the theme was not one which was native to Christianity. It is worth mentioning Justin (died 165), who rejected the idea because it did not make sense (*Dial*.4.5f.).[4] Irenaeus of Lyons (died shortly after 200), apart from other arguments (*Haer*. I.25; II.33.1f.), set over against it the view that human beings had only one life because they were created by God, and stressed the individual and personal elements; he asserted on the basis of the Bible (with Luke 16.19–31) that body and soul could not be exchanged, and thought that the migration of souls was excluded by belief in the resurrection and the judgment, which entailed the individual appearance of every human being. Finally, Tertullian (died c.220), who like Irenaeus also cited the Christian doctrine of resurrection as an obstacle (*Nat*.I,19; *De Carne Christi* 24), regarded the individuality of the soul and accordingly the final judgment as incompatible with reincarnation (*Apol*.48; *An*. 33) and found the idea of the entry of souls into animal bodies contrary and perverse (*Test.An*. 4; there is a further development of this refutation in *An*. 29–32).

That remained the state of the discussion; nothing new was added to this debate, although the theme was taken up again now and then in the fourth and fifth centuries. Even then it did not become attractive in Christianity. The African convert Arnobius the Elder at the beginning of the fourth century conceded that the philosophical doctrine of the migration of souls was a useful, deep idea which had some sense, but then rejected it because it did not fit with Christian belief in a definitive fate after death.[5] So the theme of reincarnation was not very representative of the early church.

II. Proof from the biblical writings

Since the idea of the migration of souls was introduced to Christianity from outside, anyone who advocated it in Christianity was in need of proof for it. A group like that against which Origen wrote his polemic therefore necessarily looked for proof from scripture, and indeed found it. They were convinced that Matt.11.14 (cf. 17.10) spoke of reincarnation: John the Baptist is 'Elijah who will come'; Elijah is 'back again' as John. However, the proof succeeded only in the way in which many ancient proofs from scripture achieved their aim. The idea was there from elsewhere without the text, and a text with a corresponding, often superficial, affinity to the idea could be found only if the interpreter had the relevant knowledge (here the fate of souls). The text Matt.11.14, which was preferred, does not in fact speak of souls at all and thus makes no contribution towards the idea of the migration of souls. However, the Christians whom Origen has in view[6] of course see things differently, or know better. Where it says in the Gospel that John the Baptist is to be seen as the Elijah announced for the end-time, these people, Origen reports in his Matthew commentary, know better. Where the name 'Elijah' occurs, the reference is to his soul, which has experienced a new incorporation in the body of John the Baptist. The soul of Elijah is none other than that of John. For them this is a prominent case of reincarnation, transmitted by the Bible itself. And as for proof, this is a particularly favourable case: it was Jesus himself who made the remark referred to about Elijah in the Gospel and thus in principle reported and attested the return of the soul.

The reincarnation group which Origen knows found their proof-text in Matt.11.14. The scriptural basis for the idea of reincarnation in the group concerned does not seem to have been much broader, since we may assume that otherwise Origen would have gone further to refute them and possibly would have included other texts which they used. Certainly in the Matthew Commentary, in connection with Matt.15.27f., he refers to a use of this text, which deals with animals, for the doctrine of the migration of souls, but its value is small. Furthermore, Origen even says explicitly that these people 'introduce' the dogma of reincarnation 'almost' solely from the Matthew quotation in 11.14. If, Origen says, they had interpreted the Matthew text correctly, something similar would necessarily have appeared in many other writings, in the Prophets and in the Gospels, and this is not the case.

III. The failure of the proof from scripture

Origen does not allow their proof from scripture, and at the same time demonstrates its weaknesses in many ways. His comment that there are no further instances in the Bible apart from Matt.11.14, which cannot be regarded as a proof, very much tells against such a pointed idea. The lack of evidence is enough as a refutation.

Furthermore, the scriptural proof from Matt.11.14 (see above) does not fit their doctrine. The 'migration' and reincarnation of the soul, Origen says, is understood among their followers as the consequence of sin. Because human beings sin more or less, their next incorporation will be worse or better. Therefore the prophet Elijah is a fundamentally wrong example to choose. By making his soul come into the body of John they necessarily interpret this reincarnation as a consequence of his sin, whereas the birth of John, of whom they are speaking, was announced by the same angel as announced the birth of Jesus. Accordingly they cannot mean what they say, and contradict themselves. Origen also discovers major consequences of their teaching which cause difficulties for them. If one in fact allows a reincarnation, one must immediately reckon with several, infinite series of rebirths because sin continues in the reincarnations in an open-ended way, or rather as an infinite cycle. In the commentary on Matt.17.10–13 Origen massively and repeatedly sets the end and downfall of the world over against the migration of souls, and against this end the certainty of the alien dogma shatters.

Finally, this doctrine presupposes that the soul which comes into a body brings with it a guilt from the period before birth which it has to expiate in this world. Origen does not agree with this at all (though Augustine perhaps might have done). The Christian life is about life and failure in this world. There is no crossing of horizons, as in the doctrine of reincarnation.

IV. Origen's central refutation

I have already pointed out how restrained and ultimately negative Arnobius was in speaking about the theory of the migration of souls. In his view Christian eschatology has no legitimate place for it. Others had already demonstrated this incompatibility. Origen was even more restrained. In his commentary on Matthew, because the advocates of the migration of souls whom he knew sought to prove this doctrine from the Gospel of Matthew, he had to deal with it in greater detail. But that in no way led Origen to articulate the idea of reincarnation himself in order to take it up (though, incomprehensibly, Origen is time and again regarded as the exception here among the church fathers). What he says in *Princ.* I.8.4 about reincarnation, which is continually cited for this view, clearly has an experimental character, of the kind that we know from Origen, and the text of the young Origen loses all significance when we read the clear repudiation of the migration of the souls in his Bible commentaries, which were written later. Origen himself assesses his reflections like this: 'In our view this should not be fixed doctrines, but only questions and problems. I have only addressed it so that the question touched on should not go untreated' (*De princ*.I, 8,4).[7] That is far removed from an acknowledgment of this doctrine. Origen treats the notion in terms of its intrinsic significance and inner logic, but cannot find it central and indispensable, although he goes along with the debate to the extent that he discusses the possible transmigration of human souls into animal bodies (as a punishment).

However, ultimately Origen removes the discussion of the theme of reincarnation from the agenda because his doctrinal hesitations about it clearly prevail. As with the earlier and later theologians mentioned above, for Origen eschatology is the key point. And behind eschatology lies anthropology. A soul which is created and redeemed and responsible for its career must have a final goal and destiny rather than constantly repeated incorporation. The church's doctrine of the end of the world and the judgment of the world excludes ongoing cyclical existence.[8] The Bible and the apostles know nothing of it. Where it is put forward, this happens in a form related to morality, namely that each successive incorporation is punishment or reward, and thus has to do with sin. If one in fact assumes a change of bodies for souls, then no end can be foreseen for the ever-new and further incorporations of souls, because they constantly sin yet again. Therefore the change of body for souls is continual, and indeed absolutely necessary. There is never an end to the world.

Origen himself, firmly convinced that souls pre-existed before creation, imagined that souls experience their incorporation (which happens only once) at creation as a punishment for their fall. Certainly because of the stubbornness of sin he reckons with some 'detours' for souls, but in the same body. Their bodies remain identical, but change qualitatively as reward and punishment, depending on how they come through their trials. So Origen, too, envisaged the existence of souls in patterns with a partially cyclical form, in that they repeatedly have the opportunity of a new beginning and improvement. But under the compulsion of the biblical notion of the end-time Origen sets very narrow limits to the possibility of repeating life. Nevertheless, in his doctrine, which at this point certainly remained obscure, he clearly began from a quite limited number of cycles, because otherwise the system of his theology does not 'function'. Moreover, the individuality of the human soul is confirmed under the compulsion of eschatology: it accepts its responsibility from God in a single body, i.e. in a single, unrepeatable life, and under the metaphor of the final judgment understands that human life in this world is once for all and final. Origen was firmly convinced that the notion of the migration of souls does not fit into church theology and is incompatible with it. Since the theme was of general interest at that time and was discussed in philosophy at a high level, it is remarkable that Christians did not play a larger part in the discussion. However, traces of this involvement are comparatively slight and rare. Christians gladly engaged in discourses about the soul, its nature and destiny. But the variant of reincarnation was evidently too alien in origin, and too far removed from the Christian future hope for souls, for them to want to go into it more closely.

Translated by John Bowden

Notes

1. K. Hoheisel, 'Das frühe Christentum und die Seelenwanderung', *Jahrbuch für Antike und Christentum* 27/28, Münster 1984/85, 24–46: 43; cf. U. Bianchi, 'Origen's Treatment of the Soul and the Debate over Metensomatosis', in L. Lies (ed.), *Origeniana Quarta*, Innsbruck and Vienna 1987, 270–81; H. Frohnhofen, 'Reinkarnation und frühe Kirche', *Stimmen der Zeit* 207, 1989, 236–44.

2. This by middlemen like the Greek geographer Megasthenes from the fourth/third century BCE, who himself had got as far as the Ganges.

3. E. Benz, 'Indische Einflüsse auf die frühchristliche Theologie', *Abhandlugen der Akademie der Wissenschaften und Literatur, Mainz, Geistes- und Sozialwissenschafliche Klasse* 1951, 3, 169–202: 184f.

4. Cf. most recently M. Maritano, 'Giustino Martire di fronte al problema della metempsicosi', *Salesianum* 54, 1992, 231–81: 271–81, with a large bibliography, and a systematic (today's problems) and historical (antiquity and the patristic period) treatment.

5. See L. Scheffczyk, *Der Reinkarnationsgedanke in der altchristlichen Literatur*, Munich 1985, 26f.

6. Any Origen texts not given in what follows can be found in Benz (n.3), 186–9; Frohnhofen (n.1), n.13.

7. H. Görgemanns and H. Karpp, *Origenes. Vier Bücher von den Prinzipien*, Darmstadt ²1985, 265.

8. See Scheffczyk, *Reinkarnationsgedanke* (n.5), 28–33.

Resurrection or Reincarnation?
The Christian Doctrine of Purgatory

John R. Sachs

Christian eschatology traditionally speaks of the 'four last things' (death, judgment, heaven and hell). Since the last decades of the twelfth century, it has also spoken about purgatory.[1] This doctrine, admittedly disputed among Roman Catholic, Orthodox and Protestant Christians, has significance for the urgently needed dialogue with various forms of belief in reincarnation as found both in the great religious traditions of the East and in recent New Age spirituality in the West.[2] It shows how basic Christian faith in the resurrection was later embellished and exemplifies how, despite belief in the singular finality of death and judgment (Heb.9.27), Christianity has come to acknowledge some sort of growth and development of human beings after death. Focusing on this doctrine, this article considers certain aspects of Christian hope about the final destiny of human persons and their world as a preparation for such a dialogue. The reader may thus see better where the central issues, the similarities and real differences lie with respect to his or her dialogue partner.

Certain fundamental convictions of Christian anthropology and eschatology are presumed. 1. Human beings are freely created by God and endowed with freedom in order to share God's own divine life. 2. Freedom consists in the ability to make a 'fundamental option' in and of one's life for or against God. 3. All are accountable in death and final judgment to God. 4. God's self-communication is revealed in the person of Jesus (especially in his death and resurrection) and his ministry (the announcement of God's kingdom). 5. The death and resurrection of Jesus is the revelation of the final destiny and future glory willed by God for all people and the paradigm for the Christian idea of the eternal life of the kingdom of God (heaven); 6. The only other possible final destiny for a human being is hell, which is the utter aloneness and alienation that would result from a free and complete rejection of God.

The doctrine of purgatory: official definitions

The doctrine, first defined at Lyons II (1274) and later repeated at Florence (1439) and Trent (1563), states that the souls of those who sin after baptism and having repented, die in grace before making satisfaction for their sins through worthy acts of penance, are purged after death by penalties of punishment or purification.[3] Because of the ecclesial communion with the dead, these penalties can be alleviated by the suffrages of the living faithful. Both Vatican II (*Lumen Gentium* 51) and the Congregation for the Doctrine of the Faith ('Letter on Certain Questions concerning Eschatology', 1979) have reaffirmed this teaching.

Although absent from the New Testament, the doctrine has ancient liturgical roots. *Praying for the dead*: by the second century the eucharist was offered for the dead and by the fourth century it was an integral part of the liturgy of Christian burial. *Early penitential practice*: once those who had sinned grievously after baptism could be restored to communion (after a suitable time of penance and subsequent absolution), the issue arose concerning those who died before completing their penance. It was thought that such persons could do so after death. Purgation in the hereafter was essentially seen as a continuation and completion of penance begun in this life.

In Clement of Alexandria, Origen, Augustine, Gregory the Great and the great scholastic theologians, the notion of purification and/or punishment after death was systematically developed. A few biblical texts played a key role, among them II Macc.12.28–46; Matt.5.26; Matt.12.32; and I Cor.3.10–15. In the East, purgation after death was seen as a necessary process of education and maturation preparing the soul for the vision of God. In the West, more emphasis was placed on the issues of justice and retribution, so that purgatory was viewed more in a penal context.

Understanding the doctrine

1. Purgatory need not be thought of as a place, nor has the church defined the nature or duration of the punishment and/or purgation which it entails. Most Catholic theologians view it as a *process* of final, personal confrontation between the sinful believer and God (Augustine: 'After this life, God himself is our place').

2. Those in purgatory are not in some indefinite state 'between' heaven and hell. They have died in grace, having made a free and fundamental decision for God in their lives.[4] For them purgatory is a final and sure path to heaven. It is not a 'second chance'.[5]

3. One should not think of divine punishment on the model of a civil penal system. According to Rahner, the punishment of sin is ultimately the intrinsic suffering caused by sin itself, not an additional act of retribution by God.[6] Ratzinger suggests those in purgatory are still related to history by the enduring effect of their actions on others. The guilt and suffering which go on in the world because of me are a part of me and therefore affect me. Purgatory means suffering through what I have left behind on earth.[7]

4. Because of the temporal-historical nature of human existence, the grace of repentance normally takes time to be actualized fully in all the dimensions of one's life. Even dramatic changes do not simply obliterate the past. What happens is usually a slow process of overcoming one's sinful habits, an insight exemplified in the order of penitents in the early church. Purgatory may be understood in this light as a process in which the grace of one's fundamental Yes to God in life, which becomes definitive in death, has the opportunity to penetrate all the dimensions of one's being. Since the many dimensions of human existence do not reach perfection simultaneously, it is not unreasonable to suppose that there is a full ripening of the whole person after death, or, as some theologians suggest, as a part of the process of death itself.[8] Thus, Catholic theology usually sees purgatory as a kind of process of maturation and integration.

5. Purgatory is not temporal in the ordinary sense of the word. With Augustine, we can think of it in terms of intensity rather than duration.

6. The pain of such a process arises from the suffering that sin brings of itself and from the fact that my own guilt will stand in unbearable contrast to the absolute love which God has for me and with which God wishes to fill every fibre of my being. Thus, Boros speaks of a final encounter with Christ from whose eyes the flames of perfect love (cf. Rev.1.12–17) burn through all the layers of our sin and imperfection.[9] A similar conviction guided patristic exegesis of texts like I Cor.3.10–15 and is illuminative of the traditional symbol of fire.

Important principles pertinent to the issue of reincarnation

The doctrine of purgatory is an elaboration of the basic Christian notion of resurrection, which is the central Christian symbol for the final destiny of human beings in the world. Having examined it briefly, I now present eight characteristics or principles of the Christian view of salvation that are important to bear in mind when discussing reincarnation.

1. *Theological*. Salvation comes from God, who raises the dead. Eternal life is neither the result of the immortality of the soul nor does it arise naturally out of history. It is a free and unearned gift.

2. *Historical*. Salvation is revealed and established in the history of this world and in the personal histories of all men and women. Christian life as a journey to God is founded on the faith that God has already journeyed to us, having created this world as the place of God's presence and action. Death is not merely a neutral passageway; it is an integral and finally integrating moment of one's lifetime. For me as an individual, this means that the history of my life, bounded as it is by death, is the concrete time and place of God's saving self-revelation to me. As Rahner puts it, 'In reality, it is *in* time, as its own mature fruit, that "eternity" comes about.'[10]

3. *Pneumatological*. Salvation is God's gracious self-communication to the world in love. As a sharing in God's own Spirit of life and freedom, it is at the same time forgiveness, reconciliation, peace and joy – both with God and among men and women. The new life of the Spirit begins now in the life of grace and reaches its fullness through death and resurrection in the life of glory.

4. *Christological*. Since salvation is seen as a personal relationship of love, the response of the human person is essential. For the Christian, to receive the gift of God's love means to acknowledge the reign of God and to become a disciple of Jesus. His saving action empowers and challenges us to imitate him. One must follow Jesus on the path to the cross in self-surrendering love and service in order to share in the life of the resurrection. Our actions, therefore, are of ultimate consequence.

5. *Anthropological*. Salvation touches the whole human person. Purgatory is not a purification from matter. Resurrection does not mean a departure or liberation of the soul from the body, but the liberation of the whole being, everything which one has done and become as a unique person, from sin and death. This is why the New Testament and the ancient creeds speak rather pointedly of the resurrection of the *flesh* or the *body*. At the same time it seems that, for all the care to stress the radical unity of body and soul, neither traditional (Thomistic) theology and the official doctrine dependent upon it, nor more modern approaches yet offer an anthropology and theology of resurrection which address the issue of bodiliness in a satisfactory way.[11]

6. *Ecclesiological*. Salvation touches the whole human family. As the expectation of an imminent *parousia* faded, Christian eschatology and

piety became increasingly individualistic. While eternal life is truly personal, it is not simply the progress and perfection of individuals. As symbolized by the kingdom of God preached by Jesus, it is the establishment and perfection of a universal human community of love, founded on communion with God. The resurrection of the flesh is radically connected with the whole community of believers, the body of Christ, which is a 'sacrament of communion with God and of unity among all people' (*Lumen Gentium* 1). This communion embraces both the living and the dead. In Catholic piety, even the saints are 'on the way' with the world. They have never been understood simply as those who have attained moral perfection, perfect enlightenment and ending bliss in some 'other' world. Precisely because they are completely with God, they are *with* and *for* the world. The glory of God will not reach its fullness until all flesh is raised and all creation is finally transformed.

7. *Cosmological*. Salvation embraces the whole world. This is already implied in an anthropology which sees the human person as an irreducible unity of body and spirit. This world, in its earthiest materiality and in its spirit-blessed creatures, is destined to reach its end and consummation in the resurrection 'on the last day'. This has important consequences for how we exercise our power over and responsibility for the earth and all its creatures. Thus, Christian hope in the resurrection does not look toward a promised deliverance *from* the world and its history, but for the deliverance *of* the world from sin and death, and the ripening of its time into eternity (Rahner). *Extra mundum nulla salus*. To put it pointedly: without the world, no salvation (Schillebeeckx).

8. *Eschatological*. Just as the death and resurrection of Jesus mark the inauguration of the end-time of fulfilment for history, thus giving it a radically new meaning, so too the death of the individual believer, precisely as a death in Christ, gives one's lifetime a radical depth and urgency. It is the time of God's coming and the time of human decision and response. It is the time in which one finds God and one's truest self or loses both. We live life in an eschatological 'now', without the threat or the comfort of possible repetition 'later'. What we do has eternal significance.

But it is a time marked not only by its end in death but also by its anticipation of God's merciful judgment and transforming love. For the life of the resurrection is not merely the eternal endurance of what I have accomplished in my lifetime; it is my life as graciously healed, transformed and perfected by God. For this reason, the Christian who faces death, whether as a welcome release from suffering or as the terrible unknown, all too aware of the failures, shortcomings, hopes and disappointments of his or her life, can find courage and comfort in humbly surrendering that life into the hands of God in the sure hope that the one from whom it came will bring it to fulfilment.

Notes

1. See Jacques Le Goff, *The Birth of Purgatory*, Chicago 1984.
2. See the recent analysis of the situation by André Couture, 'Reincarnation ou résurrection? Revue d'un débat et amorce d'une recherche', *Science et Esprit* 36/3, 1984, 351–74 and 37/1, 1985, 75–96.
3. At the same time, it is affirmed that some go immediately to heaven (those in no need of purification) or to hell (those who die in the state of mortal sin).
4. This 'fundamental option' is not simply taken 'before' death, since the unique encounter with God *in* death is a critical part of one's life.
5. K. Rahner, 'Purgatory', *Theological Investigations* 19, New York and London 1983, 181–93, makes the unusual suggestion that purgatory 'might offer opportunities and scope for a postmortal history of freedom to someone who has been denied such a history in his earthly life' (191), e.g., those who die as infants. Nonetheless, he presumes that 'such a definitive personal decision is certainly made in the normal case of *one* human life' (192). This might even lead to an acceptable Christian understanding of transmigration of souls as long as it were clear that reincarnation in sub-human creatures were excluded and that the final end of temporal history were not denied (192f.).
6. See K. Rahner, 'Guilt – Responsibility – Punishment within the View of Catholic Theology', *Theological Investigations* 6, New York and London 1974, 197–217.
7. See J. Ratzinger, *Eschatology. Death and Eternal Life*, Washington, DC 1988, 187–9.
8. E.g., K. Rahner, 'The Life of the Dead', *Theological Investigations 4*, New York and London 1974, 374–54: 353, and 'Purgatory', 186–92.
9. L. Boros, *The Mystery of Death*, New York and London 1965, 138.
10. K. Rahner, 'Life of the Dead' (n.8), 348. See also 'The Comfort of Time', *Theological Investigations 3*, New York and London 1974, 141–57: 'There is not only a resurrection of the body but also a resurrection of time in eternity' (156); 'Our eternity ripens out of time as the fruit in which, when it has fully grown, everything we were and became in this time is conserved' (157).
11. One significant problem for Thomistic theology and current church doctrine, which generally argue against reincarnation because of the radical unity between body and soul, is the anomalous situation of the interim state in which the soul exists separated from the body. While Thomas held that the soul as the form of the body can neither preexist its body nor transmigrate from one body to another (*Summa contra Gentiles* II,83), its substantial, intellectual nature meant that it was not dependent upon matter (*ScG* II,51). He insisted, however, upon the numerical identity of the earthly and glorified body (*ScG* IV, 84–85), which meant, in effect, that even separated from the body in the 'interim state', the soul was related to the body.
Such a realistic understanding of the glorified body is no longer intelligible. Most

contemporary writers suggest that bodiliness and the continuity of bodily identity must consist in something other than molecular identity. That seems obvious, but in what precisely they consist is far from evident.

An Anthropological Shift? The Influence of Augustine

Hermann Häring

Augustine lived at the end of an era for which the questions of reincarnation and the migration of souls were not remote. They were known in Orphism and in Manichaeism. The manifold systems of Gnosticism knew the journey of souls from heaven into the foreign land of earth and body, where they were in search of a truth to bring them on the way back to redemption. Augustine himself had sympathies with Manichaeism for many years (373–382). According to its teaching a divine spark dwells in every human being, a spark which has fallen into this world and must be restored so that it can return to its homeland. Could not this way lead through more than one embodiment? It is striking that Augustine is not concerned with this question. For a long time, too, he had no definite view of the origin of the soul.[1] It was much more important for him to respect the mystery of creation and reconciliation. We come from God and we return to God: 'No one reaches the blessed life who directs his way into nothingness or into a being which can make no one blessed.'[2] The classical scheme of departure and return is also the decisive framework for his theological thought. Here one cannot say much more than that he was in line with the theology before and after his time.

However, Augustine more than any other theologian has stamped Western Christianity down to the present day: he stands for an anthropological shift which has come up for discussion again in our day. Anyone commenting on reincarnation and resurrection must take note of this connection. What are we to adopt of Augustine's picture of human beings? Where – from a Christian point of view – are his weaknesses and problems? Can the significance of reincarnation and resurrection be explained from what he says? In connection with these questions I shall analyse four aspects which have deeply moulded the Christian view of human beings: human individualization, spiritualization and demoralization, and the neutralization of history. The analysis will show: 1. how and why the notion of reincarnation has not been adopted by a Christian anthropology, and 2. how and why the question of the resurrection must again come up for discussion.[3]

I. Individualization: human beings are their souls

'I desire to know God and the soul, otherwise nothing – nothing at all' (*Sol.* 1.2,7).

It is well known that the Augustine, born a Christian (in 354), underwent a complicated course of conversion. It was his encounter with Ambrose and a group of Neoplatonists in Milan which led to the breakthrough in 386. His decisive discovery was that God is pure Spirit and that the parallel to this in human beings is the soul. Previously he had envisaged God as a boundless corporeal mass, as an endless sea flowing round all creation.[4] It was the strict school of Plotinus which compelled him to see God in a new way: as the One and Inexpressible, identical with itself, which cannot be defined further by any designation of essence or any name and needs no relationships outside itself.[5]

Possibly Augustine overinterpreted this 'new discovery' in the *Confessions*. That God is 'spirit' may have been taken for granted earlier both by him and by the Christian tradition. However, what was less a matter of course was this strictly a-material definition of what 'spirit' means beyond time and space. Plotinus's Spirit not only transcended space and time but also entered into a relationship which was opposed to it. This Spirit was not only greater or more powerful but qualitatively different, incomparable, just the One itself. For Plotinus 'Spirit' was a hierarchical-ontological concept. By virtue of his very being God stood at the pinnacle of things. For Plotinus God was not Lord or Father, nor could God primarily be influenced in cosmic exaltation and power. For God Plotinus is primarily the supreme and the unconditioned fullness of being, enclosed in itself, and thus the decisive statement about reality itself.

Of course Augustine integrated this new experience of God into the Christian experience of God and corrected Plotinus's picture of God in many ways: one has only to read the great praise of God at the beginning of the *Confessions* (I, 4.4). There God appears not only as greatness and power, but also – in a quite un-Platonic way – as zeal and love. So this picture of God cannot be called non-Christian or un-Christian. But the new picture of God develops an unforeseeable dynamic because it is matched by a new picture of human beings. Just as God is pure spirit, so Augustine understands each individual human soul wholly as spirit. Because it is spirit, the soul can transcend the earthly, transcend the limits of space and time, and finally rest in the divine itself, yet giving human beings their identity. The decisive questions are now played out between God and the human soul, i.e. between God and the individual. Anything else has negligible significance. 'I desire to know God and the soul, otherwise nothing – nothing at all.'

But what is the soul? It is a spiritual entity, substantially shut in on itself and supporting itself, which in principle can be separated from the body. The soul can transcend space and time because it is exalted above them; it will survive death because in principle it cannot be destroyed. The Augustinian soul is the spiritual principle of human beings which – if all goes well – triumphs over the body and its needs. But that is to individualize the Christian picture of human beings. It is no coincidence that Augustine wrote the *Confessions* in the first person and in so doing laid the foundation for an individualized picture of human beings.

The influence of this picture of the soul and the human being on Western Christianity can hardly be overestimated. It intensified mystical features and time and again became the catalyst for criticism when salvation and the relationship to God were tied to church or secular institutions. At the same time this picture of human beings saw to it that salvation was time and again detached from the body, from history and from material conditions and related to an 'inner I'. It was not Augustine's Manichaeism but his Logocentrism which became a problem for later Christianity and for the whole of Western culture.

What do we conclude from this for our question of reincarnation and resurrection? The notion of the spirit-soul was received so rapidly and in such an unproblematical way because it individualized and at the same time provided ontological support for belief in the resurrection. As soul the self of the dead person had to live on after death whether it wanted to or not. Hope for resurrection was thus robbed of its provocation; the pictures of final life (despite death) were now transformed into the notions of heaven and hell. The notion of purgatory soon arose to cope with the problem of unfulfilled careers. But now, too, there was no place for the notion of reincarnation, for above everything stood the immediate return of the human self as a soul to God. Matter and body were not a form of mediation but primarily an obstacle; the first death already became the great, adequate liberation.

II. Spiritualization: rest in God

'And while we talked and panted after this eternal wisdom, we touched it in some small degree by a moment of total concentration of the heart. And we sighed and left behind us "the firstfruits of the Spirit", bound to that higher world, as we returned to the noise of our human speech where a sentence has both a beginning and an end' (*Confessions* IX, x, 24).

Neo-Platonism follows a basically mystical model. The descent of the soul into corporeality must be followed by its ascent into the spheres of the Spirit. Only there is the soul at home, can it be with itself unhindered and enjoy its due, the vision of the pure truth. Augustine experienced this ascent with his mother shortly before her death.[6] He later reports, very much in the framework of the psychology and cosmology of the time, how they left the world of the senses behind, transcended the world of the material, the earth and the stars, attained the kingdom of timeless spiritual truth and in a heartbeat made contact with wisdom itself. And in a second approach he then describes how on this way one element of sensuality after another fell away. The impressions of the senses disappeared, as did all conversation with the self; dream and fantasy-images vanished; indeed even language and all signs, riddles and similitudes were left behind. The whole universe sank into silence, since God, whom Plotinus already called Silence, can be perceived only in silence, as ultimate immediacy, without any mediation. Even vision must fundamentally be overcome, for if this vision 'could only last, and other visions of an inferior kind would be withdrawn, then this alone could ravish and absorb and enfold in inward joys the person granted the vision': this would be the eternal life that we all hope for. In the face of this expectation Monica no longer knows what she should still do in this life.

So the heart of the Augustinian Christian beats in that spiritual world. There alone is the goal worth striving for. Despite all the tasks which are to be fulfilled here, what is announced here is ultimately flight from the world, for here in the end there is no more to communicate. The world becomes a matter of indifference. The paradox and contradictoriness of this spiritualizing can be illustrated by two well-known positions of Augustine. The first asserts that in their inherited evil human beings are robbed of all freedom for the good. So it is no longer possible to communicate with the good within the world; God's grace has to do this in this world with an impotent nature. The second position asserts that evil, which for Augustine is *the* key problem of humanity and history, is ultimately nothing, is deprivation of the good.

The first position is weakened time and again in the history of Western Christianity. The many debates over original sin, grace and baptism make that clear. The second position was, amazingly, taken over unnoticed right down to the nineteenth century. Nevertheless it is astounding that evil, the great counter-force in Augustine's anthropology, ultimately has no significance. Granted, this is not a static nothingness but a nothingness which engages in dangerous plundering, a fatal nothingness. It has little to do with a liberating loss of becoming, an entrance into the womb of reality. But that this fatal nothingness ultimately has no significance before God simply indicates the triumph of a grace which cannot cope very well with this earthly world. Here God's grace does not provide freedom but replaces it.

What follows from this for our theme? Whereas Augustine's picture of the immortal soul which each individual has undermines the resurrection ontologically and thus robs it of its provocation, his flight from the world makes the resurrection a necessity of life.[8] Following Augustine, the resurrection is understood as the beginning of real life in the beyond.[9] Jacques Pohier has made the necessary critique of this objectification of a 'life after death'.[10] Certainly the resurrection is given a central significance, but the world beyond is largely excluded from its effect. It too is spiritualized. Now reincarnation would be even more a senseless course. Where God stands behind the door and God alone can help, a new life in this world would only be an inconsequential reverse. The first death is directly the way to the other kingdom 'which has no end'.

III. Demoralization: human beings were once free

'So there we again have that eternal law . . . ; it has determined with un-changeable firmness that the merit lies in the will; and reward and punishment lie in happiness and misery' (*De lib. arb*. I, 30).

For Augustine, the way to Plotinus also represents the overcoming of Manichaeism. But questions still had to be tackled. Time and again the question of the origin of evil came up. Manichaeism referred to two competing principles or gods. Augustine attacks this with all his perspicacity. Time and again he interprets the creation stories. God is the creator of all, and all that is created is God. For him any praise of God becomes a protest against this threatening world religion. He himself calls God as witness: 'All these things we see, and they are very good, because you see them in us, having given us the Spirit by which we see them and love you in them' (*Confessions* XIII, xxxiv, 49). For Augustine, any doubt in the goodness of creation is direct doubt of God's goodness. In retrospect he therefore bitterly laments the arrogance of the Manichaeans over their philosophical pseudo-solutions.[11]

But even Augustine could not close his eyes to the realities. Fundamentally he makes a radical attack on Plotinus, in whose plan of the world human freedom has no role. Plotinus explains evil as 'moving the scenery and changing the scenes, and a play of tears and laments'. Mourning and weeping do not impress him.[12] That is not the language of Augustine. He can weep, and perceives the misery of the human race. But above all he cannot allow God, who turns towards humankind in love, to will evil.

Thus Augustine's independent contribution begins with his reflection on *human freedom*.[13] In 387 he begins with his tractate *On Free Will*. This tractate, too, has a Neoplatonic stamp, but Augustine associates it firmly with the moralism which the biblical tradition has known since the prophets. The prophetic discovery is that we human beings are free before God and therefore responsible for our guilt. However, two qualifications have to be added. Augustine knows only an individual and spiritual freedom, because he anchors the possibility for evil exclusively in the will of the individual soul. In the will we come to ourselves unconditioned, for in it we decide unconditionally about God, and we need only to will this: 'Therefore nothing lies so much in our power as our will itself, since it is undividedly and uninterruptedly given into our hand, as long as we only will it.' But this is to moralize the human situation and at the same time to ask too much of it: 'Anyone who does not stand under any power cannot be overcome by any force.'[14]

That is an absolute model of freedom, but it is unhistorical and fundamentally unmerciful. There is no excuse for our willing, for in any case it is above the bonds of body and history, as a 'middle' entity between matter and spirit. Of course Augustine is not the first Christian theologian to reflect on human freedom. But individual human freedom had never before had to bear such a burden. That is understandable, since the Augustinian doctrine of freedom is now unconditionally at the service of theodicy. If God is to continue to be justified, happiness and unhappiness must be earned by human beings: they are reward or punishment. Excuses are to be unmasked as a pretext; here Job is put to silence.

Is there not again a link here with the cycle of rebirth? For under this burden must not the human soul follow a way of purification before it can appear before God? There are two reasons why this notion does not appear. First, according to Augustine's world-view, further life would only increase the guilt, since despite our freedom we are delivered over to the power of the devil.[15] The second reason is that for Augustine as for the whole of the previous Christian tradition, *God himself forgives guilt*.[16] And before God's initiative the action and the way, the kenosis and the purification of his creatures pale, whether we regard this as work or suffering. The goal guaranteed by God follows from his decision as creator, not from the order of things. Augustine emphatically developed this earliest Christian approach.

To return to Augustine's interpretation: for the sake of God's goodness he makes human beings responsible agents, for all the lines of evil now come together in their decisions. However, this stress on human freedom wreaked a bitter vengeance in Augustine's further development. As soon as he reflected on the history of humankind and caught sight of the misery and evil of the world,[17] while formally allowing his Promethean approach, in a great shift of thought from 397 on he concentrated the burden of this excessive freedom on Adam, the first great – and fundamentally the only – sinner, with whose guilt we are now hopelessly burdened, for we have all sinned in Adam (Rom.5.12b).

But what does this statement (which is exegetically wrong) mean? In a masterly analysis of Augustine's theory, Ricoeur has shown that we cannot grasp the power of evil or common guilt in a rational theory, which is what Augustine attempts to do.[18] In his own investigations into the phenomenology and symbolism of evil Ricoeur also speaks of (involuntary) stain, of tragedy, of 'imprisoned freedom' and of protest against God, and thus makes it clear that we cannot either reconstruct evil from a zero point or understand it in a unilinear way as an action freely willed.[19] Evil is always also history and future which hangs over us. It is part of the tragedy of Augustine that he wanted to balance the Christian experience of disaster rationally with a defence of God. So the emphasis on Adam's freedom led to a denial of all our freedom. The statement that we are all free thus became the assertion that we *were* all once free but can no longer struggle towards freedom before God. This freely chosen lack of freedom has ultimate significance for Augustine; he has demoralized the whole of humankind – despite resurrection and the hope of freedom. Humankind becomes the *massa damnata* in need of redemption. The catastrophic consequences of this picture of humanity – even though it was qualified time and again – for humanity is well enough known.

IV. Neutralization: the course of history

'There we shall be still and see; we shall see and we shall love; we shall love and we shall praise. Behold what will be, in the end, without end! For what is our end but to reach that kingdom which has no end?' (*De civ.Dei* XXII,30).

Augustine is not only the teacher of original sin and grace; in his monumental work *De civitate Dei* he also presented a theology of history. That may seem amazing against the background of what has been said so far. With the background of his anthropology, could Augustine still take human history seriously? Defenders could point out that Augustine took history very seriously. For him, in history a purposeful event of great drama unfolds with a clear beginning and a clear ending. Two dominions permeate each other and are engaged in combat with each other. It is not always clear who belongs to which kingdom; even the church is not simply coterminous with the kingdom of God. But Augustine looks for the distinguishing principles: 'Two kinds of love: self-love reaching the point of contempt for God, and heavenly love carried as far as contempt of self'.[20] The city of God must make a pilgrimage, threatened and unrecognized, through history. So Augustine brings together in his outline the utopia of those who believe unconditionally in God's salvation.

Nevertheless, Augustine has silenced history in a remarkable way. The earthly state, which has to care for earthly well-being, is by definition doomed to failure, because sinful human beings have already failed before their birth. With Adam's fall and banishment from paradise there begins the necessary source of sin which robs earthly history as a way to God of its force. Humankind can only go on it with outside help. In his analysis, Ernst Bloch points out that in this conception of history, nothing new, nothing unprecedented, no real liberation, can any longer take place.[21] The goal of history is as predetermined as the number of the elect.[22] And finally the course of history does not end in the fulfilment of an earthly utopia or one that is effected on earth but, as we have seen, in the vision of God in the beyond, in which we see, love and praise God. That makes history preparatory scenery. Salvation, freedom and redemption not only come exclusively from God but also remain in God. The dramatic battle here takes place against a timeless background. The history which runs its course here is fundamentally decided before it begins.

This is where the decisive shift comes. In the biblical tradition history is understood differently. There it is the primary and decisive place of God's action with human beings, not a transitional stage to the beyond. There history is the place where God frees his people, the oppressed, by teaching them freedom and liberation. From a biblical perspective history is the place where human freedom is constantly threatened afresh and can time and again be attained once more in community. Community always creates common fulfilment and common salvation.

To return to the question of resurrection: in the biblical tradition resurrection is neither ontologically a matter of course nor anthropologically necessary. It represents an intervention in history and a confrontation with it. In resurrection there is a flash of what is hidden behind every act of rescue, something unprecedented and unexpected, new, inexplicable in terms of history: fulfilment, freedom and community are possible here and now. Graves already open now. I think that it will become even clearer against this background why reincarnation represents a concept of redemption which is incompatible with resurrection.

Conclusion

Augustine is too great to be praised or rejected in a few pages. Hardly anyone will still dispute that a radical individualization and spiritualization took place in his anthropology. However, people generally overlook the central role that the human capacity for decision occupies in his work; for his theory of original sin left impotence as the only option. Therefore even the course of history does not leave room for any unexpected development. For Augustine a doctrine of reincarnation never offered itself as a solution to the problem, since the first death is necessarily the way to eternal life. But what happens if the metaphysical notion of a spirit-soul is dropped and a whole culture despairs of human freedom? Does not the course of reincarnations offer itself as an alternative model of redemption which is even acceptable to Christians?

I have my doubts. Augustine's Plotinianism has come to an end, and we can no longer understand human beings ontologically as mystical longing. Therefore it is time to see the resurrection, too, as the unexpected breakthrough of the new in our history. The prime concern is the future of this history and its people, and therefore not the individual destiny of those who seek a future in individual death. That in any case they fall into God's hands seems to me more the presupposition than the problem for a new vision of the future. Discussion with Augustine can show that the Christian hope was always directed towards resurrection, however understood. The more consistently this again becomes the vision of a final future for humankind, the clearer it will also become that reincarnation presupposes a quite different picture of human beings and their history. The decisive question is not whether the idea of reincarnation is acceptable to Christians. What is decisive is the question how the notion of endless wandering relates to hope in the God of life.

Translated by John Bowden

Notes

1. 'Whether the origin of the soul is only from descent, whether it arises anew in each newborn infant, whether it is already present somewhere and is sent by God into the body, or whether it descends to it of its own accord, of these four views of the soul we cannot affirm any directly here' (*De lib.arb.* III, 59). Augustine discusses the first possibility, so-called generationism, again in connection with the later doctrine of original sin, but without describing this doctrine.

2. Ibid.

3. The basic elements of this article derive from H. Häring, *Das Macht des Bösen. Das Erbe Augustins*, Zurich 1979.

4. *Confessions* VII; for the whole question cf. Häring, *Das Macht des Bösen*, 54–60.

5. As is well known, in Plotinus (and in Augustine's doctrine of the Trinity) a thoroughly systematic reflection is needed to explain how and why God can overcome the strict oneness to release something from himself, to be able to allow something else.

6. *Confessions* IX, x, 24–25.

7. Häring, *Das Macht des Bösen*, 181–265.

8. E. Jüngel's criticism of a necessary God must be taken up here (id., *God as the Mystery of the World*, Grand Rapids and Edinburgh 1983, 14–42).

9. 'The seventh day has no evening and no ending. You sanctified it to abide everlastingly. After your "very good" works, which you made while remaining yourself in repose, you "rested the seventh day". This utterance in your book foretells for us that after our works which, because they are your gift to us, are very good, we also may rest in you for the sabbath of eternal life' (*Confessions* XIII, xxxvi, 51).

10. J. Pohier, *God – In Fragments*, London and New York 1985, Part II.1. Pohier's positions are often interpreted as a denial of the resurrection. This interpretation is to be firmly rejected. Rather, Pohier criticizes the *reification* of belief in the resurrection which we experience universally and which among other things is based on the theory of the immortality of the soul.

11. *Confessions* V, iii.3-vii.13.

12. Häring, *Das Macht des Bösen*, 78–80.

13. This has recently been emphasized by H. Blumenberg, *Arbeit am Mythos*, Frankfurt 1979, 221f., 273 etc.

14. *De lib.arb.*III, 7; III, 19.

15. 'That man is not refused the power of the devil since he has subjected himself to his evil seduction is fully in accord with the principle of permissiveness' (*De lib.arb.*III, 29).

16. 'Thus the soul rediscovers him whom it has inwardly abandoned in its arrogance in its external world as the humble one; and if it is willing to imitate his visible humility, it rises again to that height which is invisible to it' (*De lib.arb.*III, 30).

17. Reference is usually made in this connection to Augustine's practical Manichaeism and dualistic pessimism. This may be true at the psychological level, but the argument is not enough for a theological consideration.

18. P. Ricoeur, 'Le "péché originel": Étude de signification', in *Eglise et théologie. Bulletin trimestriel de la faculté de théologie protestante de Paris* 23, 1960, 11–30.

19. Id., *Finitude et culpabilité* (two vols), Paris 1960.

20. *De civ. dei* XIV, 28.

21. E. Bloch, *The Principle of Hope* (1967), Oxford 1986, 582–90.

22. G. Kraus, *Vorherbestimmung. Traditionelle Prädestinationslehre im Licht gegenwärtgier Theologie*, Freiburg 1977.

III · Oppositions

God of History, God of Psychology

David Tracy

I. Resurrection and reincarnation

If resurrection is actual, history is real. If God raised Jesus of Nazareth from the dead, all is changed. Resurrection faith does not remove one from history but for it. The hope of human beings is not merely life after death but a hope for history itself. For the God who raised Jesus from the dead is the God who acted in the history of ancient Israel and in the history of Jesus. That same God will act in history and beyond it to save the living and the dead. The fact that God – the origin, sustainer and end of all reality – acts in history becomes the heart of Christian faith and thereby hope in history.

The great religious traditions of Hinduism and Buddhism find neither resurrection nor history at the heart of their different envisionments of Ultimate Reality and the role of *karma* in human existence. As Christians finally begin to learn from these great classical ways, we surely need a humility in understanding and learning from their central beliefs (including *karma* and reincarnation) which we have too often lacked. For example, where in all our Western speculative traditions can one find a debate as sophisticated as the many Hindu debates on the use of impersonal or personal language for naming Ultimate Reality? Even the debates focused upon Spinoza and Fichte can begin to seem relatively simple compared to the classic debates in Hinduism centred upon Shankara and Ramanuja. Even Derrida seems simplistic compared to the subtleties on the inadequacy of all language and all dialectic in the great Buddhist thinker Nagarjuna.

Or where may we find the sheer variety, even excess, in images for the divine that one finds with such abundance and power in the classic myths and symbols of Hinduism? Where can we find in all our Western traditions a more emancipatory discovery of the transience of all reality that one finds in Buddhism in all its varieties for all who can let go of their compulsive clinging? And where can modern Westerners find in their own traditions the subtle classic Hindu and Buddhist understanding of the interweaving of all human responsibilities with the cosmos itself through *karma*, rebirth and emancipation from the cycle of death and rebirth? Surely not in modern Western vulgarizations of these beliefs in 'new age' understandings of reincarnation.

It is a strange irony which we seem to face now in any serious Christian theological attempt to understand anew either resurrection or reincarnation and their real differences and similarities. At exactly the moment when some Christian theologians finally begin to listen to and study Hinduism and Buddhism with the care they so clearly need, one finds many contemporary Hindus and especially Buddhists rethinking the nature of *karma* and thereby reincarnation as well as rethinking their relationship to history. The inter-religious dialogue on these issues can seem suddenly very promising indeed (see Abe, Küng, Hick). And yet at the very moment when a genuine inter-religious dialogue could begin anew (including a serious dialogue on resurrection and reincarnation analogous to the previous ancient Greek Christian dialogue on immortality and resurrection) we may find ourselves strangely impeded for such a necessary dialogue. For the Christian hope in resurrection has too often been dissipated in modern Christianity into yet another reward for the compulsive ego empowering so much contemporary religiousness. At the same time the classic Hindu and Buddhist and even Platonic beliefs in reincarnation are surely in danger of being misunderstood at best and vulgarized at worst by being torn from their classic contexts and rethought as new hope for the same modern Western ego.

Both resurrection and reincarnation are in danger of becoming contemporary beliefs torn from their classical contexts of meaning and truth in order to become living options for all-consuming modern egos. The secret of these revisionary readings of both resurrection and reincarnation are not so hard to see: the ego is what finally counts; whatever belief helps to encourage and secure that ego will be embraced as true religion; anything which disorientates and threatens the ego will be rejected (like the God who raised Jesus from the dead and acts in history for the oppressed; like classical Hindu and Buddhist profound distrust of the ego and thereby profound misgivings on the cycle of birth, death and rebirth, reincarnation).

If a belief in God enters an ego-centred religion at all, it will be as the secret aim or projection of the ego's desires and drives. Contemporary religiousness is the ultimate triumph of Feuerbach. Religion will be approved. But resurrection of this failed Jesus of Nazareth? History as disruption? God as the dangerous God of history? All such counter-egoistic realities will quietly pass out of notice as the truly dangerous God of history passes into a no longer dangerous memory as a vague hope of our ever more distant ancestors. The question which recurs for serious Christian theologians today – the question disrupting any easy contemporary talk of resurrection or reincarnation – is, as it always was, the question of God – the God of history and the God of authentic psychology as well.

II. The hidden-revealed God of history

It is a theological commonplace that the biblical God is the God who acts in history. For the Christian the decisive manifestation of the identity of this God is revealed in the person and event of Jesus the Christ. Through Jesus Christ, Christians understand anew the reality of God as the God of history: the God who acted in the Exodus history of ancient Israel is the same God who acted and thereby decisively manifested Godself in the ministry and message, the passion, the death and resurrection of this unsubstitutable Jesus of Nazareth.

But how may contemporary Christians best understand this God who acts in the history of Jesus Christ? In one sense, modern progressive Christian theology has been an attempt to answer that question. Sometimes the answer has been divorced from the actual history of the Jesus in and through whom God has decisively disclosed the God who acts in history. The emergence of historical consciousness and thereby the development and use of historical-critical methods in the Bible has proved to be, like all human achievements, ambiguous in its effects upon modern Christian understandings of God and history. On the one hand, the results of historical-critical method have freed Christians to be both more careful and more cautious in their claims for the historical character of the events (whether Exodus, Sinai or the history of Jesus) related by the Bible. On the other hand, the use of historical-critical methods sometimes removes Christians from paying sufficient attention to the details of the history of Israel and the history of Jesus as those details were narrated by the first communities – above all, for the Christian, in the passion narratives of the New Testament.[1]

This characteristically modern loss of attention to the disclosure of the God of history in the narrative details of the passion and the resurrection narratives can be a loss, as many new narrative theologies argue, of the heart of the matter on where to look first for understanding the God of history. As the famous poetic rule observes, God is to be found in the details. Which details? For the Christian, above all, the details narrated by the first Christian communities on this Jesus they proclaimed as the Christ: the narrative details of the ministry and message, the passion, death and resurrection of Jesus of Nazareth. Who is God? God is the one who raised this disgraced Jesus from the dead and vindicated his ministry and message, his life and his person as the Christ and, as Jesus Christ, the very manifestation of who God is and who we are commanded and empowered to become. For Christians now understand themselves as commanded and empowered to find God above all in and through the historical struggle for justice and love – the historical struggle of the living and the dead – proleptically vindicated through the resurrection of Jesus.

Surely the great liberation movements and theologies of our period are the theologies which best teach us all the dangerous truth of the God of history. For the liberation theologians, starting with Gustavo Gutiérrez's brilliant reading of the Exodus narrative, know that the God of history is to be found, above all, in those great narratives of total liberation and hope.

In the liberation, political and feminist theologians, Christian theology articulates anew its faith in the God of concrete history.[2] This liberating God of history is not identical to the God of modern historical conscious-ness – a consciousness often driven by an unconscious desire to replace the biblical narratives on the God who acts in history with a modern social evolutionary narrative which may comfort modern religiousness but seems incapable of manifesting any dangerous God of concrete history.

The God of concrete history is also not identical to the God of existentialist and transcendental historicity. The latter God of historicity is disclosed by an analysis of the existential and transcendental conditions of possibility of the modern historical subject. However, this God of historicity seems far removed from the dangerous and disruptive God of the history narrated in Exodus and in the history of Jesus.

What a curious fate modern Christian theologies of history have undergone! Guided by the honest belief that they were taking history with full seriousness, many theologians began to develop either theologies of historical consciousness (Troeltsch) or theologies of historicity (Bultmann). These were and are serious and honourable enterprises. And yet the questions recur. Where is the God of history in these modern theologies of historicity and historical consciousness? Where is the history of Israel and above all the history of Jesus embedded in the biblical narratives? Where are the actual conflicts, sufferings and memories of oppression that constitute history as the struggle for justice, freedom and love? Where is resurrection as the hope for the vindication in history and beyond history of all the living and the dead? Where are the victims of history to whom the God of history narrated in the history of Jesus speaks as distinct from the victors who write the histories informing modern historical consciousness?

It would be foolish to turn against the genuine, indeed permanent, achievements of the great modern theologies of historical consciousness and historicity. In these theologies we can find the fruits of the great modern experiment: a defence of freedom and rights, an insistence on truthfulness, an honest rejection of the triumphalism of many traditional theologies of history from Eusebius through Bossuet and beyond in favour of the honest, critical, cautious correctives of traditional accounts by the use of historical-critical methods. Surely these accomplishments are the permanent achievement of modernity. However, we are now at a point in history where the underside of modernity, the dialectic of Enlightenment, must also be honestly acknowledged.

For there is an underside to all the talk about history in modern religion and theology. That underside is revealed in the shocking silence in theologies of historical consciousness and historicity alike on the victims of history. The history of modern progressive theologies of history is too often a history without radical interruption, without a memory of the victims of history, without a consciousness of patriarchy, or racism or classism or Eurocentrism, without Auschwitz, Hiroshima or the Gulag. Modern progressive theologies of history are always in danger of becoming religionized narratives of some other story than the disruptive and disturbing narrative of the fate and resurrection of Jesus the Christ.

At their best modern theologies of history articulate the great continuities of history. In this relatively optimistic account of the teleological continuities of history, modern theologies of history bear certain analogies to Luke-Acts. And yet even Luke's Gospel, with all its belief in history's fundamental continuity, adds the undertow of the inevitability of Jesus' fate best rendered in Luke by his brilliant use of the journey motif to show how Jesus must end in Jerusalem.

Many theologies of history, however Lukan in their emphasis on continuity and teleology, read history in a manner different from the more cautious Lukan narrative: history is freed of conflict and interruption and even the inevitability of suffering to become an evolutionary schema that somehow leads teleologically to Western modernity; the resurrection seems to become a purely personal, not historical, matter even as eschatology is removed from history and placed with the 'last things' of the individual; the resurrection is, in a second fatal step, divorced from the cross and its disruptive history and allowed to drift quietly into either silence or as identical to either some notion of immortality or even reincarnation.

There are, however, other theologians who have rediscovered the genuine God of history as the hidden-revealed God. For God's principal revelation is in hiddenness. This hiddenness includes, to be sure, the suffering, conflict and estrangement within the self – the dilemma of hiddenness so brilliantly articulated from Paul through Augustine, Luther, Pascal, Kierkegaard and the great existentialist theologians of our century.

However, as the political, feminist and liberation theologians imply, the principal revelation of God is not in the hiddenness of the cross, conflict, struggle, negativity.

If contemporary theology is to understand the God of history and not the God projected by its own desires for continuity and triumph, we must turn anew to the hidden-revealed God of history. The secretly evolutionary schemas in modern historical consciousness, the careless discarding of the revelatory details of the biblical narratives of the history of Jesus in favour of some new historically-reconstructed narrative of the historical Jesus, the strangely ahistorical concept of historicity of the modern subject of theology: all these theologies of the God of history must yield to the hidden-revealed God of the great biblical narratives of the God of history.

Perhaps even earlier biblical theologies of 'the God who acts in history' (von Rad, Wright) are no longer adequate to disclose the disturbing and interruptive hiddenness of the God who does act in history. For the all too continuous schemas of 'salvation-history' abstracted, above all, from the Yahwist narratives of the Old Testament and the Luke-Acts narratives of the New Testament may prove too easily co-opted by the three great corrupters of this emancipatory biblical schema: fundamentalist literalism, social evolutionary modernism or ecclesiastical triumphalism.

In biblical categories, the hidden-revealed God of history is best seen not in Luke but in the God of Mark's apocalyptic Gospel. The God of history is present through absence – as in the seeming absence of his Father to Mark's Jesus on the cross, the Jesus who cries from the cross the cry of all the victims of real history: 'My God, my God, why have you forsaken me?' This God of history is often present through absence. And yet something else also occurs in Mark's affirmation of resurrection – the seemingly absent God of Jesus' cry from the cross becomes the hidden-revealed God of the brief Markan resurrection account.

But the very reticence of Mark on resurrection united to his insistence on the centrality of cross, suffering and conflict occurs in the hiddenness of his apocalyptic vision of history as interruption, not continuity. Mark's God of history is disclosed in genuine hiddenness: the hiddenness of the conflict, struggle, negativity, suffering, cross which is actual history to the victims of history. This is the history which Mark shows to all those clear-headed enough to view history not with the eyes of the victors who write history[3] but with the new apocalyptic vision provided by the God who vindicated this Jesus whom the God of history raised from the dead. It is hardly surprising that the great liberation theologies of our day can move (as does Gustavo Gutiérrez) from the liberating historical hope for justice of the Exodus narrative to the honest wisdom in the occasional collapse of all one's hopes in Job.[4] Such a remarkable range for understanding the hidden-revealed God of history in both Exodus and Job is possible for all theologians ready to understand the God of history as the hidden-revealed God decisively manifested in the passion narratives (especially Mark) as those narratives are read in the context of the struggle of all those – living and dead – who have experienced the God of history revealed in the hiddenness of the history of Jesus – in the narrated gospel details of his ministry and message, his fate, his conflict with authorities, his table-fellowship with sinners, his suffering and fate, his cross and his resurrection.

III. The incomprehensible-comprehensible God of psychology

In the context of the revelation of the God of history in the history of Jesus of Nazareth, Christians also discover new psychological and theological understanding of the self: as a historical subject responsible to self and others before the God of history; responsible to the struggle for justice and freedom in history because capable of responding to the God of history. As the New Testament itself suggests, there are further insights into the reality of the self which Christian reflection upon the God of history and the self as a historical subject suggests. Surely Augustine and Luther, Pascal and Kierkegaard were not wrong to insist upon the introspective self as an always troubled, often estranged self living in and through the dialectic of grace and sin. That understanding of the self, unknown in its intensity of introspection to the ancients, comes to light (as Paul's great paradoxes and dialectical language show) through the dialectic of the hidden-revealed God disclosed in the history of the Crucified One. What a modern observer might name the psychological dilemmas of the self are sharpened by the harsh light cast upon the inevitability of sin and, above all, the reality of grace made available by the God revealed in the Crucified One. The God of history, properly construed, is also the God of the authentic self and thereby the God of psychology.

Nor are Christians left with only the extraordinary models for understanding the dilemmas of the self forged by Paul's great reflections on the self in the light of the hidden God revealed in the crucified one. As the Christian search for wisdom and love also becomes a search for the authentic self, Christians begin to articulate their vision of the essential self alive even in the midst of radical estrangement. At the same time, other images and understandings of God may occur to Christian reflection.

It is hardly surprising in our psychological cultures that even political, liberation and feminist theologians, without abandoning for a moment their focus on the God of history, can also engage, under the rubric of a mystical-political faith, in a further search for the true self in the light of the God of wisdom and love. Thereby does theology also turn to psychology. Here feminist theologies, with the insight that the personal is also the political, have taught all theology the deepest lessons.

As many studies have shown, modern psychology has much to teach and to learn from the great traditions of spirituality on God and the self. The classical biblical wisdom traditions as well as the later mystical traditions have returned in our period with power to deepen Christian understanding of the reality of God and thereby also the reality of the self.

This development begins, in fact, in the New Testament itself. For the movement to a wisdom reading of the history of Jesus is the great accomplishment of the Johannine tradition. Indeed it is little wonder that the classical Christian mystical traditions – the image mystics, trinitarian mystics, love mystics and apophatic mystics – will all appeal to the Gospel of John to clarify the reality of the God disclosed in the reality of the Logos.

The Johannine tradition first articulates the central Christian metaphor 'God is Love' (I John 4.8). Reflection on that metaphor will allow the wisdom and mystical traditions further insights into the interrelated realities of God, the cosmos, history and the true self. If there is a true 'God of psychology' for Christians, that God may be found only by meditation on the God of history hidden and revealed in the history of

Jesus. That God is the God of wisdom and love in-forming and trans-forming all human psychological understanding of wisdom and love taught by all those spiritual exercises faithful to the God of the Word, the Form, the Logos, the Image of Wisdom and the God who is Love.

It is true that our modern psychological culture concentrates far too much upon human subjectivity and personal experience. In that sense modern psychology can obscure not only the God of history but also the God of wisdom and love. The God of the wisdom trajectories of both Testaments and the God of the mystics does provide profound new insights into the true self. However, the wisdom traditions and the mystical traditions (and, *a fortiori*, the prophetic traditions) always place the search for personal experience and the authentic self within the context of an understanding of the God of wisdom and love and thereby the relationship not merely of the self to itself (as in modern individualism) but of the self to other, history, the cosmos, and, above all, to God. As Michel de Certeau argued,[5] there are clear historical reasons why the mystics of early modernity needed to use such person-centred subjective language in order to articulate their wisdom on the self-experiencing God. There are devastating losses whenever any psychology of individualism robs the Christian wisdom and mystical traditions of their central insight: the authentic self, for the Christian, is never an individual in the modern individualist sense but always a person with individual dignity, to be sure, but a person constituted by her/his relationships to others, to history and the struggle for justice, to the cosmos, and above all to the God of history and the God of wisdom and love. And in fidelity to that prior understanding of God Christians can speak of the God of psychology and the authentic psychological self.

From this perspective the modern development of psychology can also be construed as a positive development for the theological understanding of God and self. As Sebastian Moore has argued,[6] modern psychology can aid theology greatly by its clarification of the psychological realities of the self seeking wisdom and love grounded in meditations proper to the history of Jesus. In that sense, there is every good reason to be encouraged by the mystical and thereby also the psychological elements in the new mystical-political theologies.

In so far as Christians speak of the God of wisdom and love, they may also speak of a God of psychology. But this Christian construal of a God of psychology cannot be one more projection of the modern ego. That God could be related neither to the God of history nor to the God of wisdom and love. However, the God of wisdom and love is, for Christians, also the God who teaches new truths about the true self. Christian theologians of the patristic and mediaeval periods, for example, reflected upon intelligence as a principal clue in humans to some understanding of God as pure intelligence and wisdom.

Moreover, as Christians also reflected on the classic metaphor 'God is love' (itself grounded in the history of Jesus as disclosive of the God who is love), they found themselves more and more clearly trinitarian Christians who understood the God manifested in the history of Jesus as the only God there is – the triune God who is love. Several modern forms of theology (like Hegel and process theology) can be viewed as profound modern reflections on the intrinsically relational character of the divine reality who is love. Some post-modern forms of theology (like the powerful new theology of Jean-Luc Marion)[7] can be viewed as characteristically post-modern reflections on love not as relationality but as excess – and also as post-modern retrievals of the classic Christian neo-Platonist metaphors of God's love as overflow.

As the love of God which is excess and the wisdom of God which is ultimately incomprehensible through its very excess, a new Christian vision of God as the comprehensible-incomprehensible One has emerged once again in all Christian meditation on God. As Karl Rahner made clear in his final essays on God, God's incomprehensibility is a fully positive characteristic of God's own reality, not merely a commentary on human finitude and ignorance. Such an understanding of the incomprehensible God, moreover, frees the Christian to become, as Rahner insisted, the most radical sceptic in modernity – sceptical, above all, about modernity's pretensions to certainty – especially any presumed certainty about understanding the self through explaining its psychological processes.

The God of history, thanks to the remarkable achievements of the political, liberation and feminist theologians, can now be viewed as the God revealed in the history of Jesus, i.e., the history of the God revealed in the hiddenness of suffering, negativity, cross. By empowering human beings to become agents of history rather than either passive recipients of whatever happens or modern compulsive egos, the new vision of God also frees the 'mystical' part of the mystical-political option to its own new understanding of God as love – a love so excessive it is ultimately incomprehensible.

There is no need, therefore, to choose between history and psychology. Rather one should follow a path of disciplined spiritual exercises aiding one's understanding of the God of wisdom and love (and, in that sense, also of psychology). This spiritual path follows, not precedes, the path of discipleship to the God of history revealed in the history of Jesus. A fidelity to the fullness of that history is a fidelity to history itself as the decisive locus of God's self-revelation. In that context of the hidden-revealed God of history, all later reflections on the authentic self occur. Such reflections may be occasioned by the wisdom of the ancient Greeks or, more recently, the classic wisdom of the great Hindu and Buddhist traditions or the clear gains of modern psychologies. All wisdom from all sources should be welcomed by Christian theology as long as that wisdom is open to transformation by an understanding of the incomprehensible God of wisdom and love as that God is understood through the hidden-revealed God of history.

Notes

1. See Hans Frei, *The Eclipse of Biblical Narrative*, New Haven 1974.

2. Representative works include: Elizabeth Johnson, *She Who Is: The Mystery of God in Feminist Theological Discourse*, New York 1992; Peter Hodgson, *God in History: Shapes of Freedom*, Nashville 1989; Gustavo Gutiérrez, *The God of Life*, London and Maryknoll, NY 1991; Johann Baptist Metz, *Faith in History and Society: Toward a Practical Fundamental Theology*, New York 1980.

3. This insight into history has been articulated with power in the well-known reflections on history and its victims of Walter Benjamin, Simone Weil, and Johann Baptist Metz. It is their reflections that have most informed my own on this question.

4. Compare Gustavo Gutiérrez, *A Theology of Liberation: History, Politics and Salvation*, Maryknoll 1973 and London 1974, and id., *On Job: God-talk and the Suffering of the Innocent*, Maryknoll 1987.

5. Michel de Certeau, *La Fable Mystique*, Paris 1982.

6. Sebastian Moore, *The Crucified Jesus is no Stranger*, London and New York 1977; *The Fire and the Rose are One*, London and New York 1980.

7. Jean-Luc Marion, *God Without Being*, Chicago 1991.

The Resurrection and Christian Identity as *Conversatio Dei*

Matthew L. Lamb

The Christian faith in the resurrection of Jesus Christ from the dead asserts the fundamental victory of Christ over the powers of death. To understand how faith in the resurrection influenced Christian identity, it is important to realize how contracted the modern experience of identity has become.

Johann Baptist Metz has exposed the tyranny of the time continuum over modern consciousness and life.[1] Modern identity seems to be pinned to an ongoing continuum of time from the past through the present into the future. This evolutionary world-view is simply taken for granted as the only identity capable of living up to the demands of historical consciousness. In fact, however, it is a myth that alienates modern identity from history. For history is far more than some inexorable movement from past to future. History and human identity have been alienated into metaphors of mechanical movement under the supposed tyranny of space and time.

A striking difference between modern and pre-modern notions of identity can be seen in how we moderns identify so strangely with places and times. As an illustration, compare St Augustine's and Rousseau's *Confessions*, and St Teresa of Avila's *Life*. Augustine praises God, so that his work is an expression, as all created beings are, of God's goodness. Evil is evidence, not of any failure on God's part, but of human pride and sin. Specific dates and places do not figure significantly in Augustine's *Confessions*. Rather his entire life, with all of its stages, is woven into an intensely inter-personal dialogue or conversation with God. From the fourth to the sixteenth centuries this orientation in autobiography was consistent. Teresa of Avila's *Life* has many passages of direct dialogue with God. While there are more references to interpersonal relations with family and friends than in Augustine's *Confessions*, there is a similar attention to those realities and relations without dwelling on specific times and places.

In the eighteenth century Jean-Jacques Rousseau's posthumously published *Confessions* set the typically modern genre of autobiography, beginning each section with the relevant years, starting with his birth at Geneva in 1712. Every few pages there are specific places and dates provided. At the opening the appeal to God is not a preview of a recurrent dialogue between Rousseau and God, for that does not occur in the twelve long books. Rather it is more like an oath invoking 'my Sovereign Judge' and attesting that 'I have bared my secret soul as Thou thyself hast seen it, Eternal Being!' God is not a conversation partner in Rousseau's life, but rather a judging spectator.

All three of these texts begin with confessions of personal sins and wickedness, but in Augustine and Teresa the context is one which understands sin and evil as contractions of their conscious living, as sad and ignorant meandering from the Divine Presence with whom they are now conversing. Confession is primarily praise and joy, and the honest admission of their sins is only to manifest how gracious and compassionate God is in continuing to love and redeem them. Their self-esteem is graced, opened as it is now into the very life and love of Father, Son and Spirit. Human identity is experienced as conversational, and the most profound conversation is that between Augustine, Teresa and God. History is not movement but conscious conversation and communion. History is most profoundly prayer.

For Rousseau the confession of his wretchedness and sins is quite different, almost contrary. He is going to trump his detractors by revealing his sins in a dare with all others: 'But let each one of them reveal his heart at the foot of Thy throne with equal sincerity, and may any man who dares, say "I was a better man than he."' In effect, Rousseau initiates the modern, secular confessional genre. If a god is invoked at all, it is very much in *loco judicis*. There is no hint of a real friendship with God, only that 'He' is on a judging throne. Interpersonal relations are confined to space and time as containers and markers. Nature with its geography and chronology become the context in which Rousseau performs his egophany:

'My purpose is to display to my kind a portrait in every way true to nature, and the man I shall portray will be myself. Simply myself . . . I am made unlike any one I have ever met; I will even venture to say that I am like no one in the whole world. I may be no better, but at least I am different. Whether Nature did well or ill in breaking the mould in which she formed me, is a question which can only be resolved after the reading of my book.'[2]

Rousseau concludes his *Confessions* with the very egophanic assertion that if anyone disagrees that he is an honourable man, that person ought to be 'stifled'. For Rousseau there is the impersonal 'nature' which commands all. God is but another cipher of this cold nature. This is also an excuse mechanism. Rousseau is no longer responsible. Nature made him the way he is.

These contrasts illustrate a rather massive shift in human self-understanding, a contraction of self-presence and interpersonal conversation to those persons available to our sensations and perceptions. The dead are remembered, but they are not addressed as present in the Mystery of eternal life, as they are in Augustine and Teresa.

Reality seems increasingly restricted to what can be dated and placed. Humans are hardly made in the image and likeness of anyone else, let alone God. Rather, we humans are all locked into our own individuality within an impersonal 'nature' which removes responsibility. Identity becomes merely an epiphenomenon. It is within this context that reincarnation appeals to moderns. The time continuum will save us eventually as we pass through many lives.

Indeed, the contracted modern identity has constructed a god in its own image. Just prior to Rousseau, Newton, Spinoza and Leibniz had outlined the parameters of just such a god. Newton made space into a divine *sensorium* that permits all things to be present to God and allows God to be present in all things. Spinoza immanentized God to the point that eternity is only ideational, as in 'timeless truths'. Thinking and extending seem to be the two main attributes of God.[3]

Leibniz pushed this by often identifying perception *as* conceptualization, thereby extending the derailed cognitional theories of Newton and Spinoza even further. We are, he forcefully argued, monads. 'A genuine thing,' for Leibniz, 'must be individuated, monadized, through and through.' Leibniz's theodicy articulates a God who enables each monad to revel in egophany insofar as God is *ens perfectissimum*:

'Every substance has something of the infinite, inasmuch as it involves its cause, God; it has even some trace of his omniscience and omnipotence; now in the perfect notion of any substance, if all of its predicates are included, the necessary and the contingent, past, present, and future; indeed any substance expresses the whole world according to its position [space] and its appearance [time].[4]

What Newton termed a divine sensorium, Spinoza a *natura naturans*, and Leibniz articulated in terms of his monadology and geometrical substance philosophy, Rousseau expresses autobiographically in a language to become usual for modern narratives of the self as conscious subject. The continuum of past, present, and future, of space and time, is the context in which monads participate somehow in a divine infinity, a *sensorium divinum, Deus sive natura*, or what have you. In, through, and with the continuum of space-time all monads have their substance and participate in infinity.

Wrongly extrapolating from mechanics, Leibniz tended to equate relations with forces. If relationships are forces, then the relations that really count are extrinsic rather than intrinsic. For whatever inner forces we have, the ones to 'worry about' are those which might be stronger than ours. By the nineteenth century, references to a God were perceived as less and less relevant to modern biography, psychology, sociology and history – except as rhetorical flourish or as a symbol of pre-modern superstition.

This equation of relations with forces leads in two directions in our individualized, monadized modern world. One strand moves inward, the other outward. The inward strand delves into 'psyche' and finds in psyche the libidinal forces which 'threaten' and make a mockery of our 'thinking selves'. The superego and the endopsychic censor must tyrannically keep these libidinal and death instincts in check as best they can (Freud). Desires are 'ordered' only through forceful control, their natural state is disorder and chaos.

The other strand moves outward, to connect up with modern theories of cunning force in society and politics from Machiavelli through Hobbes, Hume and Locke to Marx and Weber. Social theory is control theory, and social power is domination (*Herrschaft*) in which those in authority give commands that are obeyed. Force is only overcome by force, so that freedom and peace, as well as order, can be guaranteed only through police and military forces. The natural state tends toward anarchy, disintegration. Laws seek to impose 'order'.

These are some of the dire consequences of the modern autobiographical identity shift. We tell our stories, neither to share in a communion with our brothers and sisters, nor to praise the reality of a gracious and compassionate God, but to engage in the competitive self-grounding or self-assertion characteristic of modern secularist contractions of conscious-ness to space and time (= objective) known with sensation and perception (= subjective).[5]

What I have been discussing until now is the aberration or cover story which, in my judgment, has tended to derail modern experiences and expressions of autobiography, of the conscious time-span in which we narrate our memories and give voice to our expectations. Modern identity to that extent is contracted, truncated to space and time. From an horizon in which a St Augustine or a St Teresa could engage in the narrative of their lives as ongoing conversations with a Divine Friend, we move to the flow of Rousseau's narrative in which God functions intermittently as a harsh judge, but in which the continuum of space and time become all important as the horizon defining reality and fact. We have seen how immediate predecessors of Rousseau had conferred a divine status on extension and duration. Soon that status could be dispensed with, just as it had in empirical science. The absence of God in modern cultures is complete. One could explore Proust's À la recherche du temps perdu as the twentieth-century apotheosis of modern autobiography become novel, as such also the longing it expresses for an eternity transcending – embracing all time. Presence seeks a time where all dates are left to the remembrance of Another.

For many the reality of events do not depend upon their being recorded exactly in place and time. Measurement and movement are not criteria for the really real. Much more reality is accorded to intersubjective presence and interpersonal conversation. Notice how mothers tend spontaneously to narrate events relative to the births of their children.

Only if instrumental rationality triumphs does the clock tend to dissociate time from human events, from interpersonal encounters. So it is not surprising that Rousseau would seek to render his narratives 'realistic' by dating and placing his memories. Modern individuality, with its monadic pretensions, underlies modern autobiography and first-person narrative novels.

Even the philosophical efforts to do justice to time and history ontologically, from Hegel through Heidegger, tend to juxtapose individu-ality and universality, Eigentlichkeit and Allgemeinheit, as though one necessarily negates aspects of the other. Objective time of universal process can be 'subject-ified' only by making the subject, with Hegel, absolutely objective Geist, or, with Heidegger, by denouncing this project as a denial of the subject's ultimate being-toward-death and finitude. In neither of these type of options is there recognized a concrete intelligibility of space and time embracing all of the extensions and durations in their concrete particularity.

The emergence of human beings with their histories marks the emergence of constitutive meaning, of human beings whose self-presence and intersubjective presence and interpersonal conversations involve a qualitatively new and different time: the time of our 'now', of our personal and communal self-presence with its memories and expectations. The human experience of time is not of discrete instants on a mechanically imagined continuum, but of a time-span which resists the easy generalizations of the empirical sciences, which is as concrete and unique as each of us in both our personal histories and in our intersubjective and interpersonal conversations. Time becomes history.

What is the *reality* of history? If historical consciousness and critical history are discoveries of modern culture, we moderns are far from having understood adequately just what it is we have discovered. Insofar as historians date events, the use of time as movement is relatively unproblematic. History raises more questions as we explore just what is real history and what is not. The point of Augustine's eleventh book of his *Confessions* is not that measurement runs up against a Neo-Kantian aporia or dilemma, but that measurement is simply unable to ground the reality of time-as-presence:

> 'It is now, however, perfectly clear that neither the future nor the past are in existence, and that it is incorrect to say that there are three times – past, present, and future. Though one might perhaps say: "There are three times – a present of things future." For these three do exist in the mind, and I do not see them anywhere else: the present time of things past is memory; the present time of things present is attentive reflection; the present time of things future is expectation. If we are allowed to use words in this way, then I see that there are three times and I admit that there are. Let us go further and say: "There are three times – past, present, and future." It is an incorrect use of language, but it is customary. Let us follow the custom. See, I do not mind, I do not object, I find no fault, provided that we understand what is said – namely, that neither what is to come nor what is past is now in existence. It is not often that we use language correctly; usually we use it incorrectly, though we understand each other's meaning.'[6]

The reality of history is glimpsed in human presence. The reality of history is known in an ongoing conversation, a dialogue down the ages, in which the time-span embraces all of humankind. By the mind Augustine does not mean a monadic, individual mind, but the individual as at one with the human species (*anima*) and all human minds. When we say that such and such a human event happened at such and such a time, we are making a historical judgment. The past event no longer exists in time. And our judgment that it either did or did not occur is based, not on our own perception of the event itself, but on a complex set of beliefs and judgments which make up historical experience. The reality of the past, as of the future, is experienced, understood, and known in the ongoing time-span of human presence.

This is not an idealism, for the present of the past is a series of sublating operations of historical experience, through historical under-standing to historical judgment. Of course, neither Augustine nor any other pre-modern knew of critical history. They did not know how to move from history as presence to the many self-correcting processes of learning which make up critical historical knowledge. In judgment the historian is not 're-enacting' the past (à la Collingwood); instead the historian is grasping that there is sufficient evidence to state that such and such did or did not occur.

When historical judgments require close attention to empirical data of sense, as in the first phase of critical history, the status of historical judgments will be the same as that of the empirical sciences. When normative historical judgments require attention to the data of conscious-ness, then it is possible to attain more than 'the best available opinion'. For mind is not simply a concept or idea, it is a reality each person in conversation embodies.[7]

The presence of the past is '*memoria*', the presence of the future is 'expectatio'; both are '*praesens*' in the present of the 'attentive reflection' constitutive of the human present. The notion of presence as memory, attention and expectation is not simply that of only one person, but, as just mentioned, of all concrete patterns of personal and communal and human species-wide operations down the ages.

Time as presence sublates time as the measure of motion. The vast expanse of extension and duration in the material universe is not, however, denigrated in a purely spiritual ascent, as with the Platonists and Manichaeans. Those who interpret St Augustine as only Platonist misread his texts.[8] No Platonist, especially a Plotinus, would, at the very height of the intellectual and mystical experience of the transcendent God, break into a prayer at how it is precisely in this experience of 'God as Truth where, O God, you feed your people Israel with the food of truth.'[9]

Indeed, Augustine makes clear how his intellectual conversion moves far beyond what any of the Platonists could sustain. For when he narrates in Book VII of his *Confessions* what he has learned from the Platonists, he never quotes them, but only Scripture.[10] We come into the presence of God in Godself, as St Augustine writes, when God speaks God's own Word to us, and in a flash of graced understanding we touch the Eternal Wisdom who creates and redeems all reality.

This intense spiritual immediacy of God is precisely the experience we shall have when we share in the Resurrection of Christ.[11] To know the reality of the Risen Christ is precisely the grace of faith which, far from darkening or blinding our intelligence, enlightens and strengthens it. As Augustine saw so clearly, only the theological virtues of faith, hope and agapic love could keep the intellectual and moral virtues from declining into Cynicism and Stoicism.

The Resurrection clearly indicates how the goodness of the material universe is present in the eternal creative and redemptive presence of God. St Augustine's grasp of God's eternal presence – an understanding that is further articulated in Boethius and St Thomas Aquinas – is neither a Platonist nor a Plotinian conception of a timeless negativity. For Augustine, God's eternal presence embraces through creation and the missions of the Son and Spirit the concrete totality of all times. There is no past and future in God, but only an eternal presence in, by, and for whom all times are created.[12] The opposition and dualism between divine eternity and time which both classical and modern philosophers have erected make it difficult for contemporary philosophers and theologians to recover the achievements of Augustine.[13]

Contrary to a Spinoza or Ricoeur, the *'Totum Esse Praesens'* or totality of existence as presence in St Augustine's understanding of God's creative and redemptive presence does *not* negate time but creates all times.[14] Far from an abstract universality of concept or thought, the eternal presence of God embraces and redeems all of creation, including the totality of human history. This is not an eternity which negates suffering. Rather, all the evil and violence brought about by sin is transformed into the only genuine kingdom of justice and love.

There are no nameless victims of history. Each and every human being is known and loved by God. And it is only such infinitely wise love that guarantees justice and mercy in the face of human evil. Far from negating human freedom, God's eternal creative presence enables human freedom. To imagine that, because God eternally knows each and every event of our lives, God thereby imposes some necessity upon us as we live and decide in history is, as Augustine, Boethius and Aquinas saw so well, a terrible category mistake. It is to imagine eternity as somehow 'before' or 'after' any event in history.[15]

The theological failure by subsequent theologians to grasp the achievements of Augustine, Boethius and Aquinas led to the nominalist abstraction of a decisionistic God, which was then later transmuted into the abstract universality of the Enlightenment 'Nature' as discussed at the beginning of this article.[16] Recent studies indicate how it is precisely the abstract universality of the Enlightenment – and not genuine Christianity – which overshadows the modern horrors such as antisemitism.[17] For only the interpersonal presence of all humans in God can constitute the concrete universality mediated in and through the particularity of each and every person, event, thing.

The concrete universality of all of history in the Triune God grounds human and interpersonal solidarity, in which each and every individual human being is understood as intrinsically related to all other members of the human species. There is no abstract notion of 'nature' as an impersonal force behind all events. This abstract 'nature' of the Enlightenment *philosophes* is the context in which human beings from other nations or races are viewed as 'others' over against those of our nation or race. The abstract nature also, as Hegel formulated so well, set the stage for the relations between one's own and the others in terms of domination and conflict.[18]

By ignoring and denigrating the specifically *theological* import of God's revelation in the Jewish and Christian covenants, modern cultures have failed to grasp that the absolutely transcendent and totally 'other' God knows and loves all of creation into being. As St Augustine and the entire Christian orthodox traditions emphasize, the whole of creation is good. Evil is not from the wholly other God, but is the product of free, intelligent creatures refusing to live as the intelligent, good and holy people God intends. All sin is a violent refusal to respond in life and praxis to the divinely willed beauty and order of creation. Bereft of this faith, modern philosophers and anthropologists have continued to ignore the distinction between human nature as good and the evil which humans commit. So all the horrors of history, all the violence that is sin and evil, are ascribed to nature. Humans are 'naturally' evil, prone to violence and crime. Only the threat and use of coercion and death can check these supposedly natural tendencies.

What Jewish and Christian revelation unfold as sin is now ascribed to nature which supposedly 'enlightened' states with secular education and law enforcement will counteract as best they can.[19] What St Augustine saw with regard to the Roman empire applies to all efforts to deal with human history apart from the theological virtues of faith, hope, and agapic love: all kingdoms seek to domesticate the '*Libido dominandi*' – the lust for domination – by the use of force and the threat of death. And so the reign of sin and domination continues.[20]

This abstract presence of nature or history is precisely *not* the divine presence revealed in the passion, death and resurrection of Jesus Christ as the Second Person of the Trinity incarnate. The resurrection cannot be affirmed apart from our faith in Christ Jesus. Like all the mysteries of our redemption, it seals our identity as ever more profoundly called to a loving conversation with the Triune God who alone can bring good out of evil, just as God alone can create. Only in the kingdom preached and incarnate in Jesus Christ do we have a kingdom of genuine understanding and love.[21]

The resurrection of the Jesus who went about healing and forgiving is the epiphany of his divine personhood. The great doctrinal distinction between nature and person indicates how all human persons are called into a communion and solidarity which far transcends the narrow confines of monadic individualism. For no one can answer the question 'Who am I?' except by narrating all the other persons from whom they were born, with whom they have lived and are living. No one can narrate who he or she is without reference to others whose being and friendship is integral to his or her own personhood. Every autobiography is *ipso facto* a heterobiography. The I and the other are in a communion whether acknowledged or not. We shall not fully understand and know who each one of us is until we understand and know each and every human person who ever has, is, or will be a member of the human race.

Understanding and knowing all human persons will then bring us to the mystery of the Word incarnate in Christ. This truly human being is a divine person. For even the totality of human persons are not fully understandable and knowable in themselves. As human persons we are all radically from Another in whom we live and move and have our being. In the mystery of the Resurrection humankind will experience the redeemed goodness of the whole of creation.

Notes

1. J. B. Metz, *Glaube in Geschichte und Gesellschaft*, Mainz [5]1992, 149ff.

2. Jean-Jacques Rousseau, *Confessions*, translated by J. M. Cohen, Harmondsworth 1985, 17, 606.

3. Cf. A. Funkenstein, *Theology and the Scientific Imagination*, Princeton 1986, 8off.; Y. Yovel, *Spinoza and Other Heretics*, Princeton 1989, 155, 213.

4. Cf. C. I. Gerhardt (ed.), *Die Philosophische Schriften von Gottfried Wilhelm Leibniz* (7 vols.), Berlin 1875-1890, Vol. 7, 311.

5. Cf. R. Rorty, 'Habermas and Lyotard on Postmodernity', in R. Bernstein (ed.), *Habermas and Modernity*, Cambridge, Mass. and Oxford 1985, 161–75.

6. St Augustine, *Confessions*, Book XI, ch.20 (my translation).

7. Cf. Bernard Lonergan, *Method in Theology*, London and New York 1972, 175–234.

8. Paul Ricoeur, *Time and Narrative*, Vols.1 and 3, Chicago 1984, 1988, offer a Neo-Kantian interpretation of Augustine's understanding of time which distorts its ontological meaning.

9. St Augustine, *Confessions*, Book IX, ch.10 with reference to Ps.79.2 (my translation).

10. Cf. James J. O'Donnell's excellent three-volume study, *Augustine Confessions*, Oxford 1992, especially Vol.II, 413. O'Donnell's work makes it less feasible to give the kind of misreading of Book VII of the *Confessions* as if it were a 'Neo-Platonic quest', as Henry Chadwick's recent translation attempts to claim.

11. *Confessions*, Book IX, ch.10 (my translation).

12. Cf. Matthew L. Lamb, 'Presence and Eternity in St Augustine' (to be published). The new readings of Augustine will indicate, for example, how the paradigm operative in Augustine is far more informed with the Jewish and Christian biblical paradigms than previously thought, cf. Johann B. Metz, 'Theologie als Theodizee?', in Willi Oelmüller (ed.) *Theodizee – Gott vor Gericht?*, Munich 1991, 113–18.

13. Cf. Professor O'Donnell's indictment: 'All of us who read Augustine fail him in many ways. Our characteristic reading is hopelessly incoherent. Denying him our full co-operation, (1) we choose to ignore some of what he says that we deny but find non-threatening; (2) we grow heatedly indignant at some of what he says that we deny and find threatening; (3) we ignore rafts of things he says that we find naive, or uninteresting, or conventional (thereby displaying that it is our taste which is itself naive, uninteresting, and conventional); (4) we patronize what we find interesting but flawed and primitive (e.g. on time and memory); (5) we admire superficially the odd purple patch; (6) we assimilate whatever pleases us to the minimalist religion of our own time, finding in him ironies he never intended; (7) we extract and highlight whatever he says that we find useful for a predetermined thesis (which may be historical, psychological, philosophical, or doctrinal, e.g. just war, immaculate conception, abortion), while not noticing that we ignore many other ideas that differ only in failing to command our enthusiasm. So when, for example, Augustine relies on the proposition that all truth is a function of Truth, and that Truth is identical with the second person of the Trinity, and that Jesus the carpenter's son is identical with that same person, we offer at most a notional assent but are compelled to interpret the idea to ourselves, rather than grasp it directly. Just when we are best at explaining Augustine, we are then perhaps furthest from his thought' (*Augustine Confessions*, n.10 above, I, xix).

14. See *Confessions*, Book XI, ch.11.

15. For a recovery of the systematic significance of Thomas Aquinas on divine presence and human freedom, cf. Bernard Lonergan, *Grace and Freedom: Operative Grace in the Thought of St Thomas Aquinas*, New York 1971.

16. Cf. Edith Wyschogrod, *Spirit in Ashes: Hegel, Heidegger and Man-Made Mass Death*, New Haven 1985, 94ff.

17. Cf. Zygmunt Bauman, *Modernity and the Holocaust*, Ithaca, NY 1989; Paul L. Rose, *Revolutionary AntiSemitism in Germany: From Kant to Wagner*, Princeton 1990; Frank E. Manuel, *The Broken Staff: Judaism Through Christian Eyes*, Cambridge, Mass 1992.

18. Wyschogrod, *Spirit in Ashes* (n.18), 106ff.

19. Cf. Anthony Giddens, *The Nation State and Violence*, Berkeley 1989; René Girard, *Things Hidden Since the Foundation of the World*, Stanford 1987.

20. St Augustine, *De Civitate Dei*, Books XIV and XIX.

21. Ibid., Book XXII.

Time without a Finale: The Background to the Debate on 'Resurrection or Reincarnation'

Johann Baptist Metz

In my view, the problem of time stands in the background of the debate on 'resurrection or reincarnation' which is carried on in this volume. Two 'messages' about time confront each other: that of Friedrich Nietzsche, with its Dionysian tone, about time without a finale, as it were the eternity of time, and the biblical, apocalyptic message of time which is limited.

The divinity of time

We know Friedrich Nietzsche as the one who proclaimed the death of God in the heart of Europe. 'God is dead' is the message of the 'madman' in Nietzsche's *Gay Science*. God is dead, and the churches are simply the 'tombs and monuments of God'.[1] What 'is', if God is dead? Looked at closely, Nietzsche's message about the death of God is a message about time. His revocation of the rule of God is the announcement of the rule of time, the elementary, inexorable and impenetrable sovereignty of time. God is dead. What now remains in all passing away is time itself: more eternal than God, more immortal than all gods. This is time without a finale, indeed – as Nietzsche explicitly emphasizes, 'without a finale in nothingness'.[2] It is time that does not begin and does not end, time that knows no deadlines and no purposes, whether heavenly or earthly, whether purposes seen speculatively as by Hegel or purposes to be realized politically as with Marx. It is time that wills nothing but itself, time as the last remaining monarch after all the metaphysically built thrones have been overthrown; time as the only post-metaphysical fascination. For millennia we had tried to form a concept of the incomprehensible God. Now in ever-new attempts we are attempting a definition of undefinable time – spurred on or irritated by Nietzsche, Heidegger, and others. It is one of the most remarkable 'signs of the time' that at present nothing is so puzzled over and reflected on, written about and argued over, than time itself.[3]

Under the spell of unfettered time

We are increasingly exposed to an anonymous pressure of acceleration, an obscure mobilization of the world in which we live. We are living under the mythical spell of time which has been released, unfettered and left to itself. Anxiety is going the rounds that in this we could even lose ourselves. 'Romanticism' is questioned in intellectual culture and the nervous cry for a 'homeland' is in the ascendant. Nietzsche, for his part, knew very well in what almost apocalyptic-seeming turbulences humanity ends up if it finally wants to bid farewell to the apocalypse, i.e. to thinking of time with a definite finale:

> 'Where are we going? Away from all the suns? Are we not for ever falling down? And falling backwards, sideways, forwards, to all sides? Is there even an above and a below? Are we not wandering as if through endless nothingness? Is not empty space breathing upon us? Has it not become colder? Is not the night and more night coming constantly? Do not lanterns have to be lit in the mornings?'[4]

Perhaps we are getting used to the diffuse atmosphere of dislocations and accelerations, used to the self-running processes in which the medium is more important than the message, and ever more rapid communication is more important than what is to be communicated. Perhaps we are getting used to the prohibitions which no one has put up publicly, but which stick all the more firmly in our heads: the prohibitions against demobilization, against lingering, against delaying. Perhaps we are becoming more insensitive to the circumstances that while we can discover more and more, we can be familiar with less and less.

The eternal recurrence of the same

Nietzsche made a proposal about doing justice to the sovereignty of time which he proclaimed.[5] To break 'the will's aversion to time', as he himself confesses, he musters his 'most abysmal ideas': the idea of the eternal recurrence of the same. The character of being is to be stamped on coming-to-be, as the supreme expression of the will to power. That is how he puts it in a note from 1885 entitled 'Recapitulation'. So passing away should be presented as constant becoming in the eternal return of the same and thus be made 'permanent'. Nietzsche's formula for Heidegger's *Being and Time* runs: "That everything returns is the most extreme approximation of a world of becoming to that of being – a culmination of contemplation."[6] That may sound abstract at first, and far removed from the everyday experience of the domination of time. But what about ideas of the migration of souls which are again preoccupying many people today? What above all about the notion of reincarnation, which is finding an increasing number of adherents? Is there not a reflection here of the suggestive power of this early Greek myth of the recurrence of the same, to which Nietzsche refers? The recent book of the German writer Botho Strauss has the displeasing title *Beginninglessness*.[7] It is a literary-aesthetic attempt at a cosmology for which the world has neither a beginning nor an end, in other words a paraphrase of the so-called steady-state cosmology[8] and the exercise of a thought and vision which forbids itself the idea of beginning and end. Evidently the theses of the beginninglessness and endlessness of the world age correspond.

Kierkegaard's protest

Kierkegaard energetically opposed the notion of the recurrence of the same. He countered it with the idea of repetitive memory. In his book on Nietzsche, Karl Löwith reports an attempt by Kierkegaard to see whether something can be repeated in such a way that the same thing recurs:

'He (Kierkegaard) had once been in Berlin and now repeats this journey to test what significance the repetition can have. He remembers how this and that had been and looked the first time; however, precisely because of his memory, he is forced to discover that nothing repeats itself but everything has changed from what it was before. The landlord and the lodging, the theatre and the whole atmosphere of the city on his first visit – everything has changed with time, and so in the new situation even the little that has remained physically the same no longer fits the different environment and so is also different from what it was before. To the extent that there is a repetition of details, it is a 'false' one, because the whole, which determines the direction of all individual details, has not remained the same. Precisely the memory of things past teaches him the impossibility of a recurrence of the same.'[9]

Memory robs the notion of the recurrence of the same of its force. So at a time in which we live less and less by memories and more and more from our reproductions, and understand them as our own experiment, we should recall the power of memory which opposes recurrence. We should resist a special kind of forgetting, that forgetting of forgetting through which the reign of a time without beginning and end establishes itself in our souls.[10]

God and time

At the heart of the biblical message there is also a message about time, a message about the end of time. All biblical statements carry a time stamp, a stamp of the end of time. In the biblical Israel we encounter a people which seems incapable of consoling and calming itself by myths or ideas. Myth ultimately seems as remote from it as metaphysics.[11] Again and again Israel turned into a landscape of cries. Israel, so talented for the here and now, so caught up in the world, did not, according to all the important evidence, believe in and think of its saviour God as outside the world, as that which is beyond time, but as the limiting end of time. This experience of God applies to the traditions of Abraham: 'I will be with you as the one who will be with you'; it applies to the prophets' message of crisis and conversion in which the landscape of Israel turns into an eschatological landscape; it applies to Job and his cry 'How long?', and finally it applies to late Old Testament apocalyptic and its theodicy which reaches deep into the New Testament. Certainly statements about the apocalyptic traditions have to be made with great care (and here I can do no more than refer to the articles about them in the present issue). Here I shall emphasize just one point: in its approach this apocalyptic is not, as critics have often suggested, a speculation remote from history, a catastrophe-driven assumption about the moment when the world comes to an end. In essence it is, rather, an attempt to disclose the limited nature of world time, an attempt to temporalize the world against the horizon of temporally limited time.

That is now also and particularly true of the history of the founding of Christianity. What theologians were later to call 'the expectation of the imminent end of the world' spans the whole New Testament scene. Jesus lived and suffered against this background and Paul formulated his christology and carried on his mission under the horizon of its understanding of time. Here for Paul the idea of time as having a limit does not mean, say, an emptying and devaluation of time and the world which appears on its horizon. For Paul time is in no way an insignificant transitional period; it is not time in the waiting room. The horizon of limited time does not mean any devaluation of the present (as is frequently suggested even in theology); on the contrary, only in it can the 'present' be experienced in that emphatic way which is characteristic of Paul. His final and irrevocable *nun*, 'now', can only be uttered against the background of limited time; under the horizon of inductively infinite time there is nothing ultimately valid, but only the hypothetical!

The apocalyptist Paul is a missionary. Without him and his missionary activity the historical project of Europe, what was later called the 'Christian West', is unthinkable. Against the horizon of limited time the world moves towards being a world of history; this specific experience of time become the root of the understanding of the world as history and thus the start of historical consciousness.

Paul the apocalyptist is also evidently in no way a fanatic about the end of the world. He does not pass over and poison the political landscape with fantasies of decline as pointed as those of the Zealots. One only has to read his sober plea for the Roman state in Romans 13 (which tends to irritate us today). The horizon of limited time does not make those who consciously live in it either voyeurs or terrorists of their own decline. Christianity became prone to totalitarianism and aggression only when it sought completely to detemporalize the apocalyptic legacy, for example by strict moralizing. That led to an apocalyptic overstraining of moral action: and it is here that the danger of fanaticism and undistanced practice lurks.

Escapism from time in theology

The way in which Christianity became theology increasingly blurred the dramatic connection between God and time as we find it in the original texts. For reasons which I shall not discuss here,[12] Christian theology has forgotten, halved, eased the tension in the temporal expression of limited time which its biblical heritage has forced on it. In the meantime it has come to live on alien, borrowed conceptions of time which make it questionable how the God of the Christian tradition could still be spoken and thought of at all in their context. Of the hidden understandings of time which are to be found in theology I would mention these: cyclical time, time framed by the pre-established cosmos; linear-teleological time, the progressive continuum to the degree that it either grows into infinity evolutionistically empty or else is dialectically delayed and interrupted; psychologized time which, as strictly biographical, has been detached from world time and natural time – and neomythical conceptions of time generally. Even in theology itself Nietzsche seems to have more opportunities than the legacy of apocalyptic, in so far as it has to serve as a programme of temporalization.

Since the days of Marcion and his dualistic axiom of the banefulness of time and the timelessness of salvation, there has been something like a permanent Gnostic temptation for Christian theology. It is accentuated today in the dualism between our lifetimes and world time. Can we still connect talk of God in any way with world time? Are we not here reverencing a secret dualism? We abandon world time to an empty, anonymous evolutionary time and seek to bring only individual lifetimes into a relationship with God. But in doing this have we not – in good Gnostic fashion - long since abandoned the creator God, and are we not exclusively venerating a redeemer God who is presupposed as being in the depths of our souls? Can a theology which holds fast to the confession of the creator God avoid the tension between cosmology and psychology, between the cosmological and the psychological conceptions of time? To say the least, it is not the individual lifetime but the time of the others, not the period up to one's own death but the experience of the death of others, which keeps eschatological unrest alive.

The anxiety in the anxieties

The mortal illness of the Christian religion is not naivety but banality. The Christian religion can become banal when in its commentary on life it only duplicates what has in any case become the modern consensus without it – and quite often against it. The naivety of biblical religion, on the other hand, lies in wait for those things which have been taken for granted. It does this, for example, by dwelling a moment longer on the texts and images of the biblical apocalypse and by enduring or holding out in their presence a little bit longer than modern consensus allows. When Christian religion returns to apocalyptic wisdom and its message of time and suspects elements of a dangerous memory here, it does not do so in order to comment on the cause of time with a *Schadenfreude* tuned to apocalypticism; it does it rather in order to detect the sources of our anxiety.

What are we anxious about? There are many alleged sources of our individual anxieties – not least also in the life of religion and the church. The advice and criticism of psychology can be helpful in detecting them and providing reassurance; it can help in making such anxieties disappear, anxieties which paralyse and intimidate, make us look small and insincere, unfree and easy to dominate . . . But is there not something like a deeper anxiety in all our individual anxieties, an anxiety which determines all of us? If we had less anxiety about our anxiety, we would presumably know more closely what really made us anxious.

It may be that archaic human beings were always made anxious by the feeling of the near end of their lives and their world; and that this mythical anxiety paralysed their work in the world. Some of this mythical anxiety also shows through in the present anxieties about catastrophes. For modern human beings, however, there is an anxiety which has become more radical – not the anxiety that everything could be ending and that for instance the planet could be doomed but, more deeply rooted, the anxiety that nothing is ever going to end any more, that there is no end. There is an anxiety that all and everything is being dragged into the surging wave of a faceless and merciless time which ultimately rolls over everyone from behind like the grains of sand on the beach and which make everything equal in the way that death does. Even a nuclear exploding planet would ultimately be delivered over to the endless death of a time 'without a finale in nothingness'. This kind of domination of time derives out any substantial expectation and gives rise to that hidden anxiety about identity which eats away the souls of modern human beings. It is difficult to decipher because it has been successfully practised for a long time under the figures of progress and development until we discover it for a few moments in the depths of our souls.

Worstward Ho!

One of Samuel Beckett's famous plays is called *Endgame*. In it one of those in the dialogue, Hamm, asks in great anxiety: 'What's happening? What's actually going on?' The other, Clov, answers 'Something or other is running its course.' These are shreds of dialogue from the tragedy of the quenching of life – the silent quenching of life without any apocalyptic cry. 'Something is running its course.' At this time without a finale human beings, human beings as we have known them so far are dying. The majesty of time proclaimed by Nietzsche as the death of God is claiming its victims. The domination of time without end is claiming the end of human beings. No one knew that better than Nietzsche himself. So he often talks about the 'abolition of mankind'; at any rate he speaks about the death of the subject, regards the subject as a mere fiction and the 'I' as well as the whole human being right up to the present as the real anthropomorphism.[13] And what about Nietzsche's dream of the new man, the exalted man, the Superman who is to be born from his message of time without a finale? Only the vision of man completely insensitive to time occurs to me, man as a smoothly running machine, man as a computerized intelligence, who does not need to remember himself because he is not threatened by any forgetting, man as a digital intelligence without history and without passion. Certainly that too would be a triumph of time over God – over God and over human beings. No finale could ever be as bad as no finale at all.

In Samuel Beckett's *Worstward Ho!* we read, 'Longing that all go. Dim go. Void go. Longing go. Vain longing that vain longing go.'[14]

Notes

1. Friedrich Nietzsche, *Werke in 3 Bänden*, Darmstadt ²1960 = ed. Schlechta I–III, here II, 126ff.

2. Schlechta III, 853 (posthumous).

3. Cf. e.g. the bibliography on time in H. Lübbe, *Im Zug der Zeit*, Berlin 1992, 25–35.

4. Schlechta II, 127.

5. For the following quotations from Nietzsche cf. J. B. Metz, 'Theologie versus Polymythie oder Kleine Apologie des biblischen Monotheismus', in O. Marquard (ed.), *Einheit und Vielheit, XIV Deutscher Kongress für Philosophie*, Hamburg 1990, 170–86, esp. 175f.; abbreviated version in *Herder Korrespondenz*, April 1988.

6. Schlechta III, 853 (posthumous).

7. Munich 1992.

8. It recalls the doctrine of the 'eternity of the world' which Augustine declared to be incompatible with the doctrine of creation. Cf. e.g. E. Behler, 'Ewigkeit der Welt', in *Historisches Wörterbuch der Philosophie*, Vol.2, 844–8.

9. K. Löwith, *Nietzsches Philosophie der ewigen Wiederkehr des Gleichen*, Stuttgart 1956, 177.

10. Cf. e.g. J. B. Metz, 'Für eine anamnetische Kultur', in H. Loewy (ed.), *Holocaust: Die Grenzen des Verstehens*, Reinbek and Hamburg 1992, 35ff.

11. For details see J. B. Metz and T. R. Peters, *Gottespassion*, Freiburg 1991.

12. Cf. my text in n.5. above.

13. For the relevant passages from Nietzsche's work cf. again n.5.

14. Samuel Beckett, *Worstward Ho*, London 1983, 36.

The Masochism of the Official Catholic Church

Masochism is the pathological phenomenon, named after Leopold von Sacher-Masoch (1836–1895), of an *individual* psycho-sexual disposition in which sexual arousement and satisfaction is achieved only through suffering ill-treatment. I am using this term in an analogous sense for a socio-psychological phenomenon to be found above all in the inner attitude and outward behaviour of those holding office in the Catholic church who shape it and exercise power in it.

The term official church is a controversial one. I am using it in a fundamentally positive sense. If one is convinced, as I am, that the things of Jesus Christ (*ta Iēsou Christou*, Philippians 2.21) should be handed down to the coming generations and preserved from oblivion, and furthermore should be given form in contemporary society, then these things of Jesus Christ need an institution, and that means people in office, men and women, ministers. It may be an exaggeration and an oversimplification, but it is not wrong to say that in a world society of the twentieth and twenty-first centuries, in which individual continents and nations are increasingly dependent on one another, it would be necessary to create a universal church government if one did not already exist.

Now the tragedy of the problem lies in the fact that the central Catholic church government as it really exists does not serve the things of Jesus as a whole; not only does it stand in the way of handing down the things of Jesus to coming generations and giving form to these things of Jesus, but in a collective masochism it does almost everything possible to cause problems and inflict suffering on many members of the Catholic church, and in so doing also to do damage to the things of Jesus. I shall go on to give five examples as evidence for the truth of this thesis.

The new '*Catechism of the Catholic Church*' is a missed opportunity.

Instead of communicating the critical and liberating content of the Old and New Testament traditions and contemporary cultures, it claims the right to impose a particular centralist Roman theology, above all with a neo-Scholastic stamp, on all Catholic Christian men and women throughout the world. Instead of bearing credible witness to people of today about the 'good news' of the irrevocable yes of the God who takes delight in men and women, on the basis of a presentation of the essentials of the biblical message, it attempts a universal indoctrination on a thousand individual questions. As if there had never been efforts at a *Foundations of Christian Faith* (Karl Rahner), or as if Hans Küng's *Credo* had never been written!

The draft text of the new moral encyclical *Veritatis splendor* basically represents no less than the attempt *formally* to resort to the pope's claim to absoluteness without an *ex cathedra* decision and without a council, when it purports to speak in accord with the bishops of the church without demonstrating this accord. In terms of *content* this text represents an attempt to extend the absolute teaching authority of the pope to ethical questions, even when the biblical traditions do not legitimate this and the basis is merely a 'natural law' as interpreted by neo-scholasticism. Many observers fear that this encyclical will merely form the basic legitimation for a second 'moral encyclical' which will then discuss concrete questions of sexual morality like birth control, homosexuality, sexual intercourse before marriage, termination of pregnancy and so on. This would be a major catastrophe for the Catholic church. That is why it is so tremendously important for the Catholic church to use what authority remains to it on behalf of a liberating, humanizing ethic based on the biblical traditions.

Sadly, the degree to which the Roman Curia has engaged in one-sided particularistic church politics throughout the world with its *nomination of bishops* is well known. Instead of observing the ancient rule of Pope Celestine I (422–432), which simply reproduces a consensus in the church of the time, namely that 'No bishop should be appointed against the will of the people', Rome has appointed a great many bishops throughout the world and forced them on church members against their will.

The current *exercising of authority* in the church largely goes against both the biblical traditions and the fundamental process of democratization in today's society. There is nothing against authority in the church! Authority is needed in the church, as in any other institution. But it must be in accord with the biblical tradition, for example that basic rule in Matthew 23.8–11: 'But you are not to be called rabbi, for you have one teacher, and you are all brethren. And call no man your father on earth, for you have one Father, who is in heaven. Neither be called masters, for you have one master, the Christ. He who is great among you shall be your servant.' So a church office which claims to itself the role of mediator between God and his people not only violates brotherly and sisterly solidarity but denies the all-embracing love of God for men and women and the effectiveness of the unique mediation of Jesus Christ.

The relationship of the institutional church to *theologians* has been disrupted. These theologians include people like Leonardo Boff, Eugen Drewermann and Hans Küng, who have a charismatic capacity to communicate the liberating message of the gospel to men and women today. And what does the institutional church do? It imposes silence on these theologians and takes away their licences. That is really perverse! Any other institution would give a fortune for people who represented it and its aims so credibly and authentically in public. And the official Catholic church forces its best people out of office.

I have given only a few examples. It would be easy to add more. Let there be no mistake about it, I do not want any fashionable, random, 'postmodern' church, adapted to the spirit of the time. And the institutional church has the right and duty to see to the continuity of the things of Jesus Christ and sometimes to raise its critical voice, to theologians as well. But above all it has the task of bearing credible witness today to the message of Jesus Christ. And that is what people are waiting for!

Norbert Greinacher

The editors of the Special Column are Norbert Greinacher and Bas van Iersel. The content of the Special Column does not necessarily reflect the views of the Editorial Board of Concilium.

Contributors

WENDY DONIGER (O'FLAHERTY) is Mircea Eliade Professor of the History of Religions at the University of Chicago. She is a past president of the American Academy of Religion, an editor of the journals *History of Religions* and *Daedalus*, a member of the academic boards of the Einstein Forum (Potsdam) and of the *Encyclopedia Britannica*, a fellow of the American Academy of Arts and Sciences, and a recipient of the medal of the Collège de France. Her many books in comparative religion and ancient Indian mythology include: *Siva: The Erotic Ascetic* (1973), *The Origins of Evil in Hindu Mythology* (1976), *Women, Androgynes, and Other Mythical Beasts* (1981), *Dreams, Illusion, and Other Realities* (1985), *Other People's Myths: The Cave of Echoes* (1988); and three Penguin Classics: *Hindu Myths* (1975), *The Rig Veda* (1980); and *The Laws of Manu* (1991). She edited the English-language edition of Yves Bonnefoy's *Dictionnaire des Mythologies*.
Address: University of Chicago, Divinity School/Swift Hall, 1025 East 58th Street, Chicago, Ill. 60637, USA.

ALOYSIUS PIERIS, a Sri Lankan Jesuit, was born in 1934. He is the founder-director of the Tulana Research Centre in Kelaniya near Colombo. A classical Indologist who has specialized in Buddhist philosophy, he is now engaged in a vast research programme on mediaeval Pali (Buddhist) philosophical literature, on which he has begun publishing a series of papers. He edits *Dialogue*, an international review for Buddhists and Christians published by the Ecumenical Institute, Colombo. He has written extensively on missiology, theology of religions, Asian theology of liberation and Buddhology. He is the author of *An Asian Theology of Liberation* (New York 1988) and *Love Meets Wisdom* (New York 1988). He is visiting professor at the Asian Pastoral Institute, Manila and has also held the Franciscan Chair of Mission Studies at Washington Theological Union (1987), the Henry Luce Chair of World Christianity at Union Theological Seminary, New York (1988) and the Ann Potter Wilson

Distinguished Chair of Theology at Vanderbilt University, Nashville (1992).
Address: Tulana Research Centre, Kohalwila Road, Gonawala, Kelaniya, Sri Lanka.

HERMANN LICHTENBERGER was born in 1943. He studied Protestant theology and oriental languages in Erlangen and Heidelberg, gained his doctorate in theology at Marburg and his Habilitation in New Testament in Marburg. From 1986 to 1988 he was Professor of Biblical Theology in the University of Bayreuth and from 1988–1993 Professor of Judaistics and New Testament in the University of Münster, Westphalia, and Director of the Institutum Judaicum Delitzschianum. He has recently been appointed Professor of New Testament and Ancient Judaism in the University of Tübingen and head of the Institute for Ancient Judaism and Hellenistic Religion. He has written much on Judaism and the New Testament and edited many academic series and journals; he is author of *Studien zum Menschenbild in Texten der Qumrangemeinde*, Göttingen 1980.
Address: Institut für antikes Judentium und hellenistische Religionsgeschichte, Universität Tübigen, Evangelisch-Theologisches Seminar, Liebermeisterstrasse 12, D7400 Tübingen 1, Germany.

DAVID S. TOOLAN SJ is an associate editor of *America* magazine in New York City and the author of *Facing West From California's Shores*, New York 1987, a study of the American consciousness movement from the 1960s to 1980s.
Address: America House, 106 West 56th Street, New York, NY 10073, USA.

JAN HEIJKE was born in Amsterdam in 1927 and is a lecturer in missiology attached to the Catholic University of Nijmegen. In addition to articles in *Spiritus, Tijdschrift voor Theologie* and *Concilium* he has written *The Image of God according to St Augustine (De* Trinitate *Excepted)*, Notre Dame 1956; *The Bible on Faith*, London 1966; *An Ecumenical Light: Taizé*, Pittsburgh 1967; *Marriage in Africa*, Brussels 1986; *Kameroense Bevrijdingstheologie: Jean-Marc Ela*, Kampen 1990.
Address: Hollestraat 30, 6612 AW Nederasselt, Netherlands.

ROGIER VAN ROSSUM was born in 1935 and entered the Congregation of the Sacred Heart in 1955; he was ordained priest in 1960. He studied missiology in Nijmegen from 1961 to 1964 and then received a grant for

field study of Afro-Brazilian religion and spiritism in Brazil. Since 1966 he has taught missiology in the theological faculty of Heerlen, which since 1992 has been fused with the theological faculty of the Catholic University of Nijmegen. His publications include *Kerk op zoek naar haar volk. Braziliaanse reisnotities* (1976) and *Waken bij die eigenheid van de ander. Evangelisering in hedendaags perspectief* (1992, with Wiel Eggen).
Address: Couberg 19, 6301 BT Valkenburg aan de Geul, Netherlands.

KARL LÖNING was born in Fürstenau, Germany in 1938. After studying German and theology he did his doctorate in New Testament exegesis. He is currently Professor of the Theology and Hermeneutics of the New Testament in the Catholic Theological Faculty of the University of Münster.
Address: Johannisstrasse 8–10, D 4400 Münster, Germany.

NORBERT BROX was born in Paderborn in 1935, and after gaining his doctorate in theology and Habilitation in patrology and ecumenical studies, became Professor of Early Church History and Patrology in the University of Regensburg. Recent publications include: *Falsche Verfassungsangaben*, Stuttgart 1975; *Der erste Petrusbrief*, Neukirchen-Vluyn ³1989; *Kirchengeschichte des Altertums*, Düsseldorf ⁴1992; *Erleuchtung und Wiedergeburt. Aktualität der Gnosis*, Munich 1988; *Der Hirt des Hermas*, Göttingen 1991.
Address: Universität Regensburg, Katholische-Theologische Fakultät, Postfach 101042, D 8400 Regensburg, Germany.

JOHN R. SACHS is a Jesuit. He gained a doctorate in theology at the University of Tübingen in 1984 and teaches systematic theology at Weston School of Theology, Cambridge, Massachusetts. Recent publications include: *Basic Christian Anthropology: The Christian Vision of Humanity*, Collegeville, MN 1991; 'Current Eschatology: Universal Salvation and the Problem of Hell', *Theological Studies* 52, 1991.
Address: Weston School of Theology, 3 Phillips Place, Cambridge, MA 02138, USA.

HERMANN HÄRING was born in 1937; he studied theology in Munich and Tübingen, where he worked at the Institute for Ecumenical Research from 1969 to 1980; since then he has been Professor of Dogmatic Theology at the Catholic University of Nijmegen. His publications include *Kirche und Kerygma. Das Kirchenbild in der Bultmannschule* (1972), *Die Macht das*

Bösen. Das Erbe Augustins (1979), and *Zum Problem des Bösen in der Theologie* (1985); he was co-editor and editorial director of the *Wörterbuch des Christentums* (1985). He has also written on questions of ecclesiology and christology, in the *Tijdschrift voor theologie* and elsewhere.
Address: Katholieke Universiteit, Faculteit der Godgeleerdheid, Erasmusgebouw, Erasmusplein, 6525 HT Nijmegen, Netherlands.

DAVID TRACY was born in 1939 in Yonkers, New York. He is a priest of the diocese of Bridgeport, Connecticut, and a doctor of theology of the Gregorian University, Rome. He is The Greeley Distinguished Service Professor of Philosophical Theology at the Divinity School of Chicago University. He is the author of *The Achievement of Bernard Lonergan* (1970), *Blessed Rage for Order: New Pluralism in Theology* (1975), *The Analogical Imagination* (1980), and *Plurality and Ambiguity* (1987).
Address: University of Chicago, Divinity School/Swift Hall, 1025 East 58th Street, Chicago, Ill. 60637, USA.

MATTHEW L. LAMB is a priest of the Archdiocese of Milwaukee. He completed his STL at the Gregorian University in Rome and his DrTheol at the Westfälische Wilhelms-Universität in Münster. He has taught at the Divinity School, University of Chicago, and the Theology Department, Marquette University, and is now Professor of Fundamental Theology at Boston College. Among his books are *History, Method and Theology* and *Solidarity with Victims*. He has also published more than a hundred and twenty articles in many journals including *America, Commonweal, Concilium, Horizons, Religious Studies Review, The Ecumenist, Method, The Lonergan Workshop Journal, Review For Religious* and *The American Behavioural Scientist*. He has also contributed chapters to many books and Festschrifts including Admund Arens (ed.), *Habermas und die Theologie*; Hans Küng and David Tracy (eds.), *The New Paradigm in Theology*, and Edward Schillebeeckx (ed.), *Mystik und Politik*.
Address: Department of Theology, Boston College, Chestnut Hill, MA 02167, USA.

JOHANN-BAPTIST METZ was born in 1928 in Auerbach (Bavaria), was ordained priest in 1954, holds doctorates in philosophy and theology, and is currently Professor of Fundamental Theology in the University of Münster. His publications include: *Armut im Geist*, 1962; *Christliche Anthropozentrik*, 1962; *Zur Theologie der Welt*, 1968 (ET *Theology of the*

World, 1969); *Reform und Gegenreformation heute*, 1969; *Kirche im Prozess der Aufklärung*, 1970; *Die Theologie in der interdisziplinären Forschung*, 1971; *Leidensgeschichte*, 1973; *Unsere Hoffnung*, 1975; *Zeit der Orden? Zur Mystik und Politik der Nachfolge*, 1977; *Glaube in Geschichte und Gesellschaft*, 1977 (ET *Faith in History and Society*, 1980); *Gott nach Auschwitz*, 1979; *Jenseits bürgerlicher Religion*, 1980; *Unterbrechungen*, 1981; *Die Theologie der Befreiung – Hoffnung oder Gefahr für die Kirche?* 1986; *Zukunftsfähigkeit. Suchbewegungen im Christentum*, 1987; *Lateinamerika und Europa: Dialog der Theologen*, 1988; *Welches Christentum hat Zufunft?* (1990); *Gottespassion* (1991); *Augen für die Anderen* (1991).

Address: Kapitelstrasse 14, D 4400 Münster, Germany.

Members of the Advisory Committee for Dogma

Directors

Johann Baptist Metz	Münster	Germany
Hermann Häring	Nijmegen	The Netherlands

Members

Rogério de Almeida Cunha	S. Joãa del Rei MG	Brazil
Ignace Berten OP	Rixensart	Belgium
Clodovis Boff	Rio de Janeiro	Brazil
Leonardo Boff OFM	Petrópolis	Brazil
Anne Carr	Chicago, Ill.	USA
Fernando Castillo	Santiago	Chile
Yves Congar OP	Paris	France
Karl Derksen OP	Utrecht	The Netherlands
Severino Dianich	Caprona/Pisa	Italy
Josef Doré	Paris	France
Bernard-Dominique Dupuy	Paris	France
Donal Flanagan	Maynooth	Ireland
José González-Faus	Barcelona	Spain
Anton Houtepen	Utrecht	The Netherlands
Elizabeth Johnson CSJ	Washington, DC	USA
Joseph Komonchak	Washington, DC	USA
Nicholas Lash	Cambridge	England
René Laurentin	Evry-Cedex	France
Karl Lehmann	Mainz	Germany
James McCue	Iowa City, Iowa	USA
Carlo Molari	Rome	Italy
Heribert Mühlen	Paderborn	Germany
Peter Nemeshegyi SJ	Tokyo	Japan
Herwi Rikhof	Nijmegen	The Netherlands
Josef Rovira Belloso	Barcelona	Spain
Luigi Sartori	Padua	Italy
Edward Schillebeeckx OP	Nijmegen	The Netherlands
Piet Schoonenberg SJ	Nijmegen	The Netherlands
Robert Schreiter CPpS	Chicago, Ill.	USA
Dorothee Sölle	Hamburg	Germany
Jean-Marie Tillard OP	Ottawa/Ont.	Canada
Tharcisse Tshibangu Tshishiku	Kinshasa	Zaire
Herbert Vorgrimler	Münster	Germany
Bonifac Willems OP	Nijmegen	The Netherlands

Concilium

Issues of Concilium to be published in 1994

1994/1: Violence against Women

Edited by Elisabeth Schüssler Fiorenza and M. Shawn Copeland

This issue aims not only to raise church consciousness about the existence of widespread violence against women but also to explore its significance for a feminist rearticulation of Christian theology. Accounts of women's experiences of violence are followed by discussions of cultural identity values, including the pornographic exploitation of women; a third part discusses the church's encouragement of violence against women and the issue ends with new means of feminine empowerment.

03024 2   February

1994/2: Christianity and Culture: A Mutual Enrichment

Edited by Norbert Greinacher and Norbert Mette

This issue explores that point in the relationship between Christianity and cultures where a culture discloses new dimensions of the gospel as well as being the object of criticism in the light of the gospel, a process known as 'inculturation'. Part One examines fundamental aspects of inculturation, Part Two looks at test cases (in Coptic Christianity, Zaire, Pakistan, Latin America and Canada) and Part Three reflects thinking on inculturation.

03025 0   April

1994/3   Islam: A Challenge for Christianity

Edited by Hans Küng and Jürgen Moltmann

The first section describes experiences of Islam in Africa, Central Asia, Indonesia, Pakistan and Europe and the second the threat felt by Christians from Islam and by Muslims from Christianity. The final section explores the challenges posed by Islam; monotheism, the unity of religion and politics, Islamic views of human rights and the position Islam occupies as a religion coming into being after Christianity and Judaism.

03026 9   June

1994/4: Mysticism and the Institutional Crisis

Edited by Christian Duquoc and Gustavo Gutiérrez

The decline in mainstream church membership suggests that a less institutional and more mystical approach to religion is called for, and that this is an approach which the churches should encourage. This issue looks at mystical movements in various parts of the globe, from Latin America through Africa to Asia, and asks how they can become less marginalized than they have been in the past.

03022 7   August

1994/5: Catholic Identity

Edited by James Provost and Knut Walf

How is an institution, a movement, a social teaching, or even an individual 'Catholic' today? The question has many applications, in terms of identity, discipline, teaching and so on. This issue explores its ramifications with relation to particular theological and canonical issues.

03028 5   October

1994/6: Why Theology?

Edited by Werner Jeanrond and Claude Jeffré

This issue surveys the programme, methods and audience for theology today, at a time when its status as an academic discipline is no longer possible, and in many contexts it cannot be engaged in without interference from state and church authorities.

03029 3   December

Back Issues of *Concilium* still available

All listed issues are available at £6.95 each. Add 10% of value for postage.
US, Canadian and Philippian subscribers contact: Orbis Books, Shipping Dept.,
Maryknoll, NY 10545 USA
Special rates are sometimes available for large orders. Please write for details.

1965

1	Dogma ed. Schillebeeckx: *The very first issue*
2	Liturgy On the Vatican Constitution: *Jungmann and Gelineau*
3	Pastoral ed. Rahner: *The first issue on this topic*
4	Ecumenism: *Küng on charismatic structure, Baum on other churches*
5	Moral Theology: *Its nature: law, decalogue, birth control*
6	Church and World: *Metz, von Balthasar, Rahner on ideology*
7	Church History: *Early church, Constance, Trent, religious freedom*
8	Canon Law: *Conferences and Collegiality*
9	Spirituality: *Murray Rogers, von Balthasar: East and West*
10	Scripture Inspiration and Authority; *R.E. Murphy, Bruce Vawter*

1966

11	Dogma Christology: *Congar, Schoonenberg, Vorgrimler*
12	Liturgy: *The liturgical assembly, new church music*
13	Pastoral Mission after Vatican 2
14	Ecumenism: *Getting to know the other churches*
15	Moral Theology Religious Freedom: *Roland Bainton, Yves Congar*
16	Church and World Christian Faith v. Atheism: *Moltmann, Ricoeur*
17	Church History: *Jansenism, Luther, Gregorian Reform*
18	Religious Freedom In Judaism, Hinduism, Spain, Africa
19	Religionless Christianity? *Bernard Cooke, Duquoc, Geffre*
20	Bible and Tradition: *Blenkinsopp, Fitzmeyer, P. Grelot*

1967

21	Revelation and Dogma: *A reconsideration*
23	Atheism and Indifference: *Includes two Rahner articles*
24	Debate on the Sacraments: *Thurian, Kasper, Ratzinger, Meyendorff*
25	Morality, Progress and History: *Can the moral law develop?*
26	Evolution: *Harvey Cox, Ellul, Rahner, Eric Mascall*
27	Church History: *Sherwin-White and Oberman; enlightenment*
28	Canon Law - Theology and Renewal: *Hopes for the new Canon Law*
29	Spirituality and Politics: *Balthasar; J.A.T. Robinson discussed*
30	The Value of the OT: *John McKenzie, Munoz Iglesias, Coppens*

1968

31	Man, World and Sacrament: *Congar, J.J.Hughes on Anglican orders*
32	Death and Burial: *Theology and Liturgy*
33	Preaching the Word of God: *Congar, Rahner on demythologizing*
34	Apostolic by Succession? *Issues in ministry*
35	The Church and Social Morality: *Major article by Garaudy*
36	Faith and Politics: *Metz, Schillebeeckx, Leslie Dewart*
37	Prophecy: *Francis of Assisi, Ignatius of Loyola, Wesley, Newman*
38	Order and the Sacraments: *Confirmation, marriage, bishops*

Please send orders and remittances to:
SCM Press Ltd, 26-30 Tottenham Road, London N1 4BZ

Concilium Subscription Information - outside North America

Individual Annual Subscription (six issues): £30.00

Institution Annual Subscription (six issues): £40.00

Airmail subscriptions: add £10.00

Individual issues: £8.95 each

New subscribers please return this form:
for a two-year subscription, double the appropriate rate

(for individuals)   £30.00   (1/2 years)   . . . .

(for institutions)   £40.00   (1/2 years)   . . . .

Airmail postage
outside Europe +£10.00   (1/2 years)   . . . .

Total . . . .

I wish to subscribe for one/two years as an individual/institution
(delete as appropriate)

Name/Institution . . . .

Address . . . .

. . . .

. . . .

I enclose a cheque for . . . . payable to SCM Press Ltd

Please charge my Access/Visa/Mastercard no. . . . .

Signature . . . . .Expiry Date . . . .

Please return this form to:
SCM PRESS LTD 26-30 Tottenham Road, London N1 4BZ

CONCILIUM

The Theological Journal of the 1990s

Now Available from Orbis Books!

Founded in 1965 and published six times a year, *Concilium* is a world-wide journal of theology. Its editors and essayists encompass a veritable "who's who" of theological scholars. Not only the greatest names in Catholic theology, but exciting new voices from every part of the world, have written for this unique journal.

Concilium exists to promote theological discussion in the spirit of Vatican II, out of which it was born. It is a catholic journal in the widest sense: rooted firmly in the Catholic heritage, open to other Christian traditions and the world's faiths. Each issue of *Concilium* focuses on a theme of crucial importance and the widest possible concern for our time. With contributions from Asia, Africa, North and South America, and Europe, *Concilium* truly reflects the multiple facets of the world church.

Now available from Orbis Books, *Concilium* will continue to focus theological debate and to challenge scholars and students alike.

Books available from Orbis Books

Disposable People?

The Plight of Refugees

Judy Mayotte

Relates the story of refugee peoples from Afghanistan, Cambodia and Ethiopia in the context of their countries' tortured sociopolitical and economic histories.

'Filled with emotion as well as fact ... will become a classic in its field' (*Liv Ullman*).

ISBN: 0 88344 839 4   cased   368pp   index   bibliography

The Cosmotheandric Experience

Emerging Religious Consciousness

Raimon Panikkar

The scholar who has lived and worked on the boundaries between West and East, Hinduism, Buddhism and Christianity; philosophy, science and theology; describes the arrival of new ways of intuiting reality. The cosmotheandric experience denotes an essential intertwining of the cosmic, the human and the divine - all interpenetrating dimensions of a single whole.

ISBN: 0 88344 862 9   cased   150pp   index

Faith and Culture series

Asian Faces of Jesus

edited R.S. Sugirtharajah

Today, Asians are seeking the face of the original Jesus - his Asian face. This work provides an overview of the most creative new christologies from Asia. Contributors include Ovey N. Mohammed, Seiichi Yagi, Aloysius Pieris, Stanley J. Samartha, Michael Amaladoss, C.S. Song, Kosuke Kayama, Michael Rodrigo, Chung Hyun Kyung and Sebastian Kappen.

ISBN: 0 88344 833 5   paper   250pp   index
(outside North America, order this title from SCM PRESS London:
ISBN: 0 334 01878 1   paper)